Soundings

D1739769

Issue 14

One-
dimensional
politics

EDITORS
Stuart Hall
Doreen Massey
Michael Rustin

THEME EDITORS
Michael Rustin
and Wendy Wheeler

POETRY EDITOR
Carole Satyamurti

REVIEWS EDITORS
Becky Hall and
Susanna Rustin

ART EDITOR
Tim Davison

EDITORIAL OFFICE
Lawrence & Wishart
99a Wallis Road
London E9 5LN

Soundings is published three
times a year, in autumn,
spring and summer by:
Soundings Ltd
c/o **Lawrence & Wishart**
99a Wallis Road
London E9 5LN
Email: soundings@l-w-bks.demon.co.uk

ADVERTISEMENTS
Write for information to Soundings,
c/o Lawrence & Wishart

SUBSCRIPTIONS
1999 subscription rates are (for three issues):
UK: Institutions £70, Individuals £35
Rest of the world: Institutions £80, Individuals
£45

ISSN 1362 6620
ISBN 0 85315 923 8

Text setting Art Services, Norwich
Cover photograph: ©Ute Klaphake

Printed in Great Britain by
Cambridge University Press, Cambridge

CONTENTS

——————————— Continued on next page ———————————

Continued from previous page

NOTES ON CONTRIBUTORS

Paul Aylward and Mark Hayes are authors of the research paper 'Anti-Fascist Action: An Ethnographic Investigation into an Organisation on the Periphery of politics'.

Isaac D. Balbus teaches social and political theory at the University of Illinois at Chicago, He is the author of *Emotional Rescue: The Theory and Practice of a Feminist Father*, Routledge 1998.

Anne Briggs is an adoptive parent who lives and works in London.

Shereen Benjamin and Cynthia Cockburn are members of the Raised Voices, a London based political choir.

Dave Byrne is Reader in Sociology and Social Policy at the University of Durham. He is author of *Complexity Theory and the Social Sciences* (1998) and *Social Exclusion* (1999).

Helen Crowley teaches Women's Studies at the University of North London.

Laura Dubinsky works as a trade union organiser in the United States.

Susanne Ehrhardt works as a doctor for Oxfam. A selection of her poems was published in *New Chatto Poets II*.

Stephen Frosh is Professor of Psychology at Birkbeck College, University of London, and Consultant Clinical Psychologist at the Tavistock Clinic.

Judith Kazantzis regularly visits Key West and New Mexico. She has published eight collections of poems, of which the latest is *The Odysseus Poems*, a new look at ancient heroism.

Maureen Mackintosh is Professor of Economics at the Open University.

Joan Michelson's poetry and prose has been widely published in the UK and the USA. She teaches Creative Writing and Holocaust Studies at the University of Wolverhampton.

Fabian Peake is a practising artist and teaches fine art at Manchester Metropolitan University. His poems have been widely published in Britain and the United States.

Mario Petrucci is currently poet in residence at the Imperial War Museum. His work has won many awards, including the 1999 Bridport poetry prize, and his collection, *Shrapnel and Sheets* was a Poetry Book Society Recommendation

Gavin Poynter is Head of the Department of Innovation Studies at the University of East London. He has recently completed a book on management reform, workplace relations and the restructuring of the UK services sector.

Dave Renton teaches history at Edge Hill College. In 1999, he worked as a visiting lecturer at Rhodes University in South Africa. His next book, *Marx on Globalisation* will be published by Lawrence and Wishart in the spring.

Barry Richards is Professor of Human Relations at the University of East London. This essay is based on part of his recent inaugural lecture there.

Joanna Rosenthall is a couple psychoanalytic psychotherapist at the Tavistock Marital Studies Institute. She also writes fiction, including short stories.

Michael Rustin is Professor of Sociology and Dean of the Faculty of Social Sciences at the University of East London. He is co-editor of *Soundings* magazine.

Wendy Wheeler is Reader in English Literature in the School of Arts and Humanities, University of North London, and author of *A New Modernity? Change in Science, Literature and Politics*, Lawrence and Wishart 1999.

Where are we now?

The pervasive power and scope of capitalist social relations provides a magazine like *Soundings* with much to criticise and qualify. The left in its various forms is principally engaged these days in such criticism, whether in relation to very broad phenomena such as globalisation, or more locally - for example in relation to the apparent endorsement of capitalism as a way of life by the New Labour government in Britain. Our theme for the second half of this issue, *One-Dimensional Politics*, characterises an invasive market monoculture as a central issue, and points to alternative ways of thinking which have potential for development.

It is, however, a serious problem for the left that it is uncertain any longer of what alternatives to the present order it stands for. The effects of the collapse of Communism in Europe, and of the end of the Cold War, are still potent and deep-seated. The prolonged failure of internal reform in state socialist Russia and Europe leaves room for doubt that a benign, organic evolution of this system was possible, desirable as it was. In reality, the defeat of this 'revisionist' possibility of reform in the east was a blow to the democratic left everywhere, even when, as often, its opposition to authoritarian communism was a defining principle of its separate existence as a democratic or libertarian left. This defeat, rendered decisive, if not final, by the events of 1989, had the consequence of removing any substantial global alternative to the regime of capital.

This victory for capitalism also greatly lessened the risk of world war and nuclear destruction, an unqualified good, and it has opened up political spaces within the dominant global system which has made possible many changes for the better. It seems unlikely that the ANC would have found itself in government in South Africa, without catastrophic conflict and disruption, if the broader global threat of Communism had not already been almost at its end. Fred Halliday presciently suggested, soon after the transition of 1989, that several peripheral conflicts which were in effect theatres of the Cold War would now be capable of negotiated settlement; and so, in this general lessening of tension, it has proved. Even the government of Angola now seems somewhere near the point of defeating its barbarous Unitá enemy, this now having at last lost the support of its former South African and United States allies. Creeping moves towards settlements between Syria, Israel and the Palestinians, and even perhaps the resolution in Northern Ireland, are related to this change of climate. Judgements about interventions are no longer being made solely in terms of a global balance of power - though these issues remain decisive in some regions, such as the Balkans. Instead, such mundane considerations as whether or not a territory offers opportunities for profitable investment have acquired more weight in deciding what levels of intervention are deemed necessary by the American government and its allies. Similarly, within the metropolitan countries, the defeat of the left, in the large, and the replacement of many governments of the right with those of the centre, has reduced the necessity for the left to be persecuted. The moderate left can even be permitted to achieve some small gains, though small they certainly are.

It is however little consolation to the left to be tolerated largely because it is harmless. (New Labour continues to fight its battle against it with undiminished zeal, but representing Ken Livingstone as an extremist or revolutionary does not make him into one.) The deep question the left faces is to know what it fundamentally stands for, and to know what vision it now has for a society that is not to be for ever predominantly capitalist. Redefining its maps of potential change, in both society and politics - the former the larger sphere - is now the fundamental task of the 'thinking left'.

Soundings has been trying to address these questions since its launch. It has worked on this positive part of its task in a polymorphous way, sphere by sphere or fragment by fragment. We won't repeat here why we decided that this would be a more fruitful strategy than attempting to devise a unified theory or programme, but we have no regrets about having done so. Our Theme issues on *Windrush Echoes*, *Transversal Politics*, and *Emotional Labour* ('bringing feelings back in') are just four examples of our explorations of new agendas. *Active Welfare* discussed whether the idea of participatory democracy could be given an embodiment in everyday welfare practices. A memorable article showed that even patients who had been severely mentally ill could take a great deal of responsibility for a democratic process of consultation, if public services had a sufficient commitment to this. *Windrush Echoes* explored the transformation of Britain over fifty years into a multi-ethnic nation, and the new conceptions of nation, race, identity and home that this has initiated. *Transversal Politics* argued for new ways of approaching differences - ethnic, religious, or political - and the conflicts that are often focused on them. It reported new kinds of democratic practice, based on the sharing of experience across boundaries of conflict, and on the learning and understanding that can come from this. *Emotional Labour* drew attention to a new dimension of exploitation in work settings; and the discussion about emotional labour made it possible to identify a site of new demands and aspirations - for the recognition of emotional needs and fulfilments, as well as of prospective injury. There will be a *Soundings* conference on this topic, later this year (we will send subscribers details), and we will also return to this topic in these pages.

Demands for human recognition and reciprocity are fundamental to a new radical agenda, and much of the work of *Soundings* has implicitly or explicitly been about these and their denial. The universalist egalitarian demands of the traditional left, necessary as they were, were in certain respects one-dimensional and 'flattening' - of claims to individual difference, but also of ideas of social and cultural variety. Virtual cultural homogeneity (which is, confusingly, defined as consumer choice) is an inherent project of capitalism, and calling this into question is one of the first tasks of its critics. Fundamental to these debates about recognition have been the spheres of gender and ethnicity, and the kinds of understanding and values relevant to each. These central issues of modern radical politics have never fitted comfortably into traditional socialist formulations, constructed as these inevitably were by social movements at a particular historical moment, and bounded as these were by implicit assumptions of race, gender, and nation. It is now one of the primary tasks of radical thought to attempt to clarify the relation between the necessary equalities and uniformities of all human beings (of civil, political and economic rights) and the recognition of desirable spheres of difference - and their necessity for authentic self-development.

Soundings has hitherto published little explicitly theoretical discussion, though there has been much implicit theoretical reflection in its pages - for example about the Third Way. This was an early choice made from a commitment to avoid academicism, and from a wish to engage more directly and accessibly with experience, which we have also explored through poetry, documentary writing, and fiction. Wise or not as this choice against theoretical writing may initially have been, we recognise that it has had some costs. The socialist tradition, and its 'new left' variant from which *Soundings* derives, has always been intensely theoretical. It has sought to construct general models and explanations, as a guide to understanding the world, and the kinds of social action which are possible within it. And though 'theory' can be an academic substitute for, or retreat from, 'action', it does not have to be. Indeed, without it - and this is one of the left's contemporary problems - there can be no sufficient orienting principles or 'maps' at all.

We need to take stock, both as a magazine, and as a wider radical community, of those ideas and theories which can provide illuminating ways of thinking. One example of such work is that of Manuel Castells, whose remarkable trilogy, *The Information Society*, is the most comprehensive and sustained analysis and critique of informational capitalism to have been produced in recent years. In the absence of an engaged theoretical debate, there is a risk that powerful work like this can be appropriated not as a critique of the global system, but as an apparent argument for its inevitability. This indeed has happened with the concept of globalisation, as we have been trying to show in these pages. This is an imbalance we propose to redress. We shall be seeking in future explicitly to identify theoretical resources for critique, resources which can aid the construction of new social imaginaries, alternatives to the present global order.

Finally, *Soundings* needs to be more profoundly international, and non-European, than it has been. It is not that this dimension has been lacking - there have been special issues on *States of Africa*, and *The European Left*, and we have published many individual articles (including two in the current number) which focus on countries other than Britain. But the issue is larger than the balance of articles on this or that topic. The truth is that a radical politics today has to be global in its essence. What happens in South Africa, or Jamaica, or Mexico, or India, is equally as defining for the future of any radical political or cultural project in Britain as anything that happens in Paris, Berlin or London. Ecologically, this is now obvious. A global environmental catastrophe now threatens, as a result of unregulated economic growth. Culturally and economically, if not yet politically, there is in fact one world only. Our problem is that the market system has come to understand, and adjust to this fact, much more quickly than the left has. This is another issue that *Soundings* will be addressing more fully in future.

We would like to hear from readers who would like to write for *Soundings*, or suggest topics, articles or themes for it. We hold discussion meetings from time to time, though hitherto these have been mainly for contributors. Readers who would like to have notice of these should contact the *Soundings* office, by post or email.

MR

Organising where it is needed

First generation immigrant workers in North America

Laura Dubinsky

Laura Dubinsky describes recent initiatives by North American unions to organise those workers who are most marginalised and therefore most in need of unions.

Organising to survive

Unions are waking up to the realisation that they must either organise or slide into irrelevance. Threatened by a loss of members and political power, unions in the United States, Britain, Australia, and to a lesser extent Canada, are redirecting resources into organising. Unions have also learned that they need to bring in immigrants and workers of colour if they are to survive. 'Three out of four [British] unions say that they are specifically targeting Black and Asian workers as part of their recruitment programmes', according to the TUC. [1] 'The ranks of the American labour movement cannot increase significantly without

---

1. TUC *organising report*, November 1998.

12

Latino workers', [2] says the AFL-CIO. The Canadian labour movement wishes to 'emphasise organising in its broadest sense, recognising the changing faces in our communities.'[3] Wherever unions are recommitting to organising, officials are talking about the need to organise more workers of colour.

However, while pledges at union congress are easily made, organising *any* workers requires enormous effort and internal change from unions. What exactly do unions need to do if they want to organise, for example, first generation immigrants? In what ways will campaigns for first generation immigrant workers differ from other campaigns and what are the winning strategies for organising immigrant workers?

This article describes the fight to organise immigrant workers in North America and suggests that traditional perceptions of immigrant workers as frightened and quiescent are misplaced, as are notions that the difficulties of organising immigrant workers primarily arise from cultural difference. With immigration levels at their highest levels in fifty years in both the United States and Canada, American unions and certain private sector unions in Canada which are experiencing sharp declines in numbers have engaged in a wave of campaigns to organise immigrant workers. As these unions have found, first generation immigrants often have *every* reason to want a union but the very factors that make them eager to mobilise (they are concentrated in the economy's worst jobs, in sectors where employers are trying to keep labour costs down) also make the campaigns to organise them exceptionally tough and conflictual. Campaigns to organise immigrants are high stakes fights. Immigrant workers are often desperate to win workplace rights and changes; but their employers, facing intense competition from other low-wage firms, are willing to go to extreme lengths to keep the union out and labour costs down. Not only does the union have to develop new and appropriate strategies to organise and represent immigrant groups who are traditionally under-represented in the ranks of union membership and union staff; the union also has to become enough of a fighting movement to win the formation of the new union branches for immigrant workers, and to deal with the new members' painful and pressing workplace problems.

---

2.   AFL-CIO press release, 23 August 1996.
3.   Canadian Labour Congress, *Organizing Policy Statement*, May 1999 Convention.

In North America, immigrant workers have shown the capacity for mobilisation on a mass scale which can bring unions the sheer numbers they need to survive; and the tough nature of the campaigns to win recognition and workplace changes for immigrant workers is also forcing those unions which are seriously engaged in organising them to be especially active and combative. Although many unions are organising as much to prevent extinction as for ideological beliefs, the nature of their new members may force change upon them: a more active and responsive relation to their members, and a readiness to take risks to defend the rights of those in the worst jobs the economy has to offer.

Immigrant workers and the union

There are two misconceptions which are popular among unions contemplating organising for the first time among new groups of immigrant workers. The first misconception assumes that immigrants are quiescent and hard to organise and that patient organisers must painstakingly coax immigrants to overcome their fear and natural suspicion of unions. 'They're *different*, how will we talk to them? Do they have papers? Will they be afraid?' Yet, in the early years of the century, recent arrivals working in bad jobs, with a poor grasp of English, helped found several major American and Canadian unions, and now, again, immigrants are pushing their unions into unsought-for militancy.

The second misconception is more a half-truth: it says that cultural differences are what stand between immigrant workers and unions. If unions can help immigrant workers identify with unions, by hiring immigrant organisers and representatives, allying themselves with immigrant community groups and adopting culturally sensitive organising strategies, then immigrants will join unions. 'It is imperative that workers can connect their own experiences with representatives of the union and the union's overall image. It's important to know that someone has shared the difficulties of working, being discriminated against, and marginalised in the broader society.' [4]

Unions involved in organising immigrant workers have certainly needed to

---

4. 'Feminist Organizing Models: No Easy Recipe, building the diversity and strength of the labour movement', CLC Women's Symposium, November 1998. http://www.clc-ctc.ca/woman/femorg.

respond to the particular needs of new members - who speak another language, experience racism inside and outside the workplace, operate in another cultural context, and on occasions have problems in obtaining legal immigrant status. However, adapting to these differences is not enough to establish a successful organising programme which can bring in large numbers of new members, retain the new members and continue to grow. As well as appropriate and creative tactics to remodel the union's image into one immigrants can identify with, immigrants *also* require that their unions act like real unions and deal effectively with their problems as exploited, low-wage workers.

Militant workers

Far from being timid or requiring gentle hand-holding, immigrant workers have proved open to unionisation. In United States union recognition elections, unions have been more successful in units with a majority of workers of colour [5], and immigrant workers have been involved in many of the recent high-profile campaigns. In the last decade, SEIU, the service employees union, has organised over 35,000 janitorial workers across the United States, most of them Mexican and Central American. HERE, the hotel and restaurant employees' union, is organising 7000 Latino and Asian hotel workers in the Los Angeles area. USWA, the steelworkers union, organised over 5000 workers in light manufacturing and in call centres in Ontario in 1999, many of whom were immigrants. Brad James, USWA organising director in Ontario emphasises that, 'Punjabis, Filipinos and Tamils are the dominant engine of the steelworkers' organising program in Ontario'. The United Auto Workers, another union rarely associated in recent years with low-wage immigrant workers, just organised 1200 workers, all Mexican women, at an auto-parts plant in Detroit. UNITE, the garment and textile workers' union for which I work, has been organising Haitian and Latino nursing home workers in Florida; Latino manufacturing workers in the American Southwest; and Asian and Haitian manufacturing workers in Canada. This year, UNITE has organised over 10,000 Latino laundry workers around the United States.

Why would a group of workers who are relatively new to the country and

---

5. Kate Bronfenbrenner, in K. Bronfenbrenner, S. Friedman, R. Hurd, R. Oswald, R. Seeber, *Organizing to Win: New Research on Union Strategies*, 1998, p32.

its working environment, whose legal and working situation may be precarious, and who have every reason to believe that organising will provoke a vicious employer response, take these risks? Immigrants are not a homogenous group: not all immigrants are willing or able to organise. Just like their native-born counterparts, many immigrants are too terrified, too fragmented or just too uninterested to form a union. However, it does seem, based on the recent wave of immigrant organising, that many immigrants have more to gain from organising than other workers, more anger driving them to organise and more capacity for mass mobilisation. Their concerns are often the same as those of native workers - pay, benefits, fair treatment, a say at work, safety - but amplified by the discrimination which puts them in bad jobs and keeps them there.

Immigrants have abundant economic reasons to organise: most immigrants are low-wage workers, struggling to make ends meet at the bottom of the economic pile, their job prospects circumscribed by lack of language proficiency, unfamiliarity, labour market discrimination and sometimes documentation problems. It has been calculated that the new immigrants to the United States will be unable to catch up with the earnings of native workers within their lifetimes. The average man who migrated to the United States between 1975 and 1979 will, even after forty years, still earn 12 per cent less than a comparable native worker. [6] In Canada, the average Latino worker makes 19 per cent less than the average native worker. [7] At the bottom of the economic ladder, there is everything to win and sometimes little to lose by fighting for better wages, treatment and conditions. Overall, American union workers earn 32 per cent more than non-union workers; but African American union members make 45 per cent more than African American non-members and Latino union workers earn 54 per cent more than their non-union counterparts. [8] Although low-wage workers lack a savings cushion if dismissed during a union fight, a minimum wage job is also the easiest to find.

There are also important non-economic gains which immigrants can expect from union membership. Union contractual language which may be taken for granted by white workers makes a vital difference for immigrant workers, indeed

6. George Borjas, *Friends or Strangers*, 1990, p45 .
7. George Borjas, *International Differences in the Labour Market Performance of Immigrants*, 1988, pp12, 44.
8. Bureau of Labour Statistics data 1998.

all workers of colour, in reducing discrimination. A standardised pay structure prevents white and non-white workers being paid different rates for the same job. A non-discrimination clause backed up with a grievance procedure provides a recourse for the worker who has again and again been allocated the worst machine, the worst shift or the last choice for vacation. A watertight job bidding procedure ensures that the good, well-paid jobs go to the most senior workers and not simply the white workers.

However, workers are motivated to take the risks entailed in organising not only by rational calculations about the benefits of union membership, but by frustration, even rage, over the way they are treated, and a desire to regain some control over their working lives. Workers organising in the face of employer opposition must be angry enough to challenge someone with the power to take their job away. Immigrants often have more to make them angry: the daily humiliations of being snubbed by supervisors, being treated differently from others with comparable skills, being arbitrarily disciplined. Especially in situations where class boundaries are visibly demarcated, and management and workers literally speak different languages, immigrant workers are often acutely aware of class differences and exploitation: they have few illusions that the boss has their best interests at heart or that, if they sit tight, one day they too can become the boss.

For immigrants faced with stark injustice, the union is frequently the first organisation that provides a hope for change. Other forms of political participation being restricted, many immigrants see in the union a means to challenge injustice in the wider society as well as in the workplace. Here are some examples from signed articles that Cape Verdean workers submitted to their union newsletter during a UNITE organising drive in their auto-parts factory in Rhode Island, USA [translated from Portuguese]:

> We can't say anything if we don't like what they say to us. I want the union so they can realise that, without us, this company wouldn't exist. When they speak to workers, we feel discrimination very clearly. They are everything and we are nothing. Every time they open their mouths, words come out that mean discrimination.

> The time has come to open our eyes to the truth. It is the moment to speak

and to shout. It is the moment to feel liberty. Many people think that the union is just about benefits and money, but that's not it. The union is the voice of THE WORKERS. IT IS TIME TO SPEAK AND TO SAY GOODBYE TO FEAR.

Immigrants are helped in their organising struggles by the value placed on collective protest in certain immigrant groups and by the dense networks that bind them together. Many Central American immigrants and refugees in California, and many Tamils and Bangladeshis in Ontario and Quebec, arrive with prior experience of left-wing activism. The networks of family and social ties, and community and political organisations, that bind together first generation immigrants even in the most sprawling metropolitan area, help them stick together to combat their employer. When Tamil bookbinders organised with UNITE in Toronto, all but one of the 89 Tamil workers showed up for their union meeting, having organised car-pools. Every one of the Tamils was later found to have voted for the union, including the lone Tamil who was in a well-paid skilled job, who had received many persuasive late-night phone calls from his friends and relatives.

Militant employers

With these pressing motives and particular capacities to organise, what is holding immigrant workers back: why have more immigrants not joined unions already? Just as immigrant workers have much to win through unionisation, their employers often have a lot to lose. Immigrant workers are disproportionately concentrated in private sector low-wage service jobs, and in unskilled manufacturing and agricultural jobs, in which union density is low and labour costs are frequently a high proportion of overall costs. These industries are also often structurally difficult to organise (with elaborate subcontracting arrangements, ease of relocation for labour-intensive manufacturing, or small dispersed units). Unsurprisingly, it has been found that low-wage firms and firms in industries with low union density are more likely to pursue union avoidance strategies. [9] These are not employers who are likely to be reaching out to legitimate unions to enter partnership agreements. Accepting the union means

---

9. John Lawler, *Unionization and Deunionization*, 1990, pp70-71.

driving costs up in the long term; on the other hand, these employers may find it worthwhile and 'cost-effective' to run a vicious anti-union campaign: firing workers from unskilled jobs is cheap because they are easily replaced.

In addition to the rational cost calculations that employers make in opposing unionisation, there is also, especially in family-owned businesses, an irrational response that can keep an employer fighting the union long after the fight has become more costly than giving in. This personal injured-pride response is particularly strong where the employer is racist and has always complacently believed that their employees 'don't even know what a union is'. The employer is *outraged* at the idea of having to deal with immigrant workers as equals across the bargaining table, or as shop-stewards, and may pursue the anti-union fight even at the risk of endangering the business. At the Toronto bookbindery mentioned earlier, management was confident up until the moment of the recognition ballot that the Tamil workers could not possibly want a union. When they got over their shock at the results of the vote, the management locked the workers out, reopening only after having lost several important clients.

Brutal campaigns, high hopes

Immigrants' uphill fight to form unions is further complicated by North American labour laws which provide ample opportunity for employers to impede unionisation. In Canada and the United States, unions are usually formed in three steps: winning recognition, obtaining the contract, and forming the local union branch. At each step, the costs for immigrant workers and their unions are high, requiring additional commitment, resources and activism from the union.

Just winning recognition is a baptism of fire for workers in North America. In the United States, 30 per cent of the workers of a given workplace must sign cards of interest in the union; around 6 weeks then elapse before the National Labour Relations Board holds an election to determine whether a majority supports recognition. By the time workers vote on whether to join their union, management, under advice from specialised attorneys, will have leafleted the workers, shown them videos, spoken to them one-on-one and in meetings, put up posters, handed out anti-union buttons and t-shirts, held special company picnics, formed an anti-union committee and, not infrequently, fired selected workers. Management will have let workers know, in carefully couched terms, that in joining the union they risk losing their job, closing the plant down, or winning nothing while paying a fortune in union dues - but that if the union leaves, management is ready to solve the workers' problems. At the Rhode Island auto-parts factory mentioned earlier, 80 per cent of the primarily Cape Verdean workers signed union cards. Six weeks later, after 13 per cent of the workforce had been fired, the workers voted against the union.

In Ontario, where the lag between obtaining the necessary cards and voting is only a week, and in Quebec, where a majority on cards is sufficient to avoid a vote, employers have less response time. However, what Canada does have is legal wrangles, which may last months, over the constitution of the bargaining unit - whose card or vote counts. Whether in the United States or Canada, the tougher the employer, the more resources the union will have to commit. Conflictual campaigns mean more organisers working to leap the complex legal hurdles and reach a majority as fast as possible, and higher legal costs to cover fights to stop employer intimidation, reverse unfair dismissals, or simply define the bargaining unit.

When workers actually win recognition in North America, they have got through weeks of employer intimidation or months of legal obfuscation, buoyed up by hopes that their working lives are about to change. Winning recognition is a euphoric moment: for activists from dirty, unrewarding jobs, it can be an unparalleled feeling of achievement. Visiting foreign trade union officials have sometimes been taken back by the evangelical fervour of American union activists, but if they had to go through the same things to obtain recognition, they would probably also run shouting and screaming through the streets when they won! All these high hopes mean the union must now move fast to bargain for improvements.

The second step of winning a contract is usually even harder. Especially in the United States, employers intent on keeping labour costs down can drag out negotiations for months, even years. In the United States and Canada, immigrant workers and their unions have struck, demonstrated, occupied buildings, blocked bridges, stormed managers' country clubs and cocktail evenings - all in pursuit of the signature on the dotted line. However, if the union has embarked upon a recognition campaign haphazardly, in response to workers' desire to organise, without strategic consideration for the ability to win workplace improvements, obtaining a collective agreement may in fact be impossible. Many immigrants work in industries - such as subcontracted garment manufacture, or cleaning contractors - where no matter how much the workers want the union, unless the union has a strategy to organise across the industry and take wages out of inter-firm competition, no stable union organisation can be formed. 'Hot-shopping' - randomly organising wherever workers are willing, without an industrial strategy - leads to situations where the union wins recognition at a low-wage employer only to realise that fulfilling the workers' expectations means closing the company down.

'when workers actually win recognition in North America it is a euphoric moment'

Even where the union manages to ratify a good contract, with economic gains and substantial new rights and protections, the fight is not over. An employer who wants to fight the union tooth and nail can still continually attempt to violate the contract, discipline union activists and whittle away at the union's strength and credibility. The benign neglect too often displayed by unions towards shop floor problems is disastrous at this stage: if workers are getting fired, pregnant women are being denied chairs to sit on, workload is being increased, worker leaders are being threatened with immigration red tape, a union official cannot just pop by once a month. Immigrant workers' problems being worse and more immediate, the union must complete the third step of forming an autonomous local branch, with worker leaders trained both as representatives and as organisers capable of calling shop floor protests. The full-time official representative allocated to the newly organised workplace must also remain unusually responsive and available.

The risks and costs for unions organising any workers, but especially those at the bottom of the labour market ladder, are considerable. If the union falls short of the expectations of workers who have organised in the face of major obstacles, and fails to react effectively to their urgent problems, it will find it difficult to retain the new members, and risk seeing future recruitment in that ethnic group and area dry up. The same tight networks that help immigrants organise in the first place also spread news fast about the union's behaviour towards its members. However, the rewards for the union - as well as the workers - can also be high. If new members have a sense of ownership over their local union branch, and perceive that their union has been ready to fight for them when necessary, there is the potential for a dynamic, growing movement. If the union has credibility among that ethnic group, it will become one of the first organisations to be called when there is a problem in an unorganised plant, and the activists from the earlier campaign will become volunteer organisers on new campaigns.

Organising in practice

Who are the unions trying to organise in this explosive context of militant workers, intransigent employers and predominantly anti-union labour laws? Two of the unions at the forefront of organising immigrant workers in the North American service and manufacturing sectors are the Service Employees International Union and the Union of Needletrades, Industrial and Textile Employees. Both unions spend almost 50 per cent of their annual budget on organising. John Sweeney, the AFL-CIO president elected in 1995 on a slate of organising 'at an unprecedented pace and scale', is from SEIU. His talk of 'blocking bridges whenever employers turn a deaf ear' comes directly out of the high-profile civil disobedience waged by his union during the Justice for Janitors campaign among Latino janitors. UNITE, though born out of the struggles of first generation immigrants in the early years of the century, has spent the last decades organising primarily - against enormous odds - in the textile mills and the white and African American small towns of the anti-union states of the American South and Southwest. Recently, UNITE has begun to modify its own model for organising in urban areas with high immigrant concentrations.

'Days of Rage': SEIU in Washington DC

The Service Employees International Union, originally the Building Service Employees International Union, was formed by immigrant workers and African Americans in Chicago in 1920. During the 1930s depression, janitorial unionism spread, reaching Washington DC and other major cities, and encompassing both public sector work and work in privately owned buildings.

The structure of janitorial work in commercial real estate is based upon contractors who hire out labour to building owners. Although the contractors are technically the janitors' employers, the power and the money resides with the building owners, who have the discretion to switch from union to non-union contractors in pursuit of cheaper services. Non-union companies sprang up during the 1970s and 1980s in response to the union's push to improve wages and working conditions. Many of these contractors were offshoots from larger union companies, operating non-union under another name.

In the mid 1970s, the fight over working conditions and union power in commercial janitorial jobs came to a head in Washington DC with an industry-wide strike. The union lost the strike and SEIU's Washington DC local 82 was almost wiped out, retaining only its public sector membership. Commercial janitorial work in Washington was now entirely non-union, passing from being a decent job to a minimum wage job. Meanwhile, the demographics of commercial janitors underwent a transformation: while local 82's remaining membership and staff were predominantly African American, the new low-wage, non-union workers entering the commercial janitorial labour market were almost entirely Mexican and Central American.

Beginning with a struggle in Pittsburgh in the mid 1980s, SEIU began 'Justice for Janitors', a nation-wide struggle to organise commercial janitors. Because of its urban, low-wage base, the major JforJ campaigns have involved Latino workers; however, local 82's organising director, Maria Naranjo, points out that, 'our strategy is based upon the industry, not the fact that it employs immigrants. We would use the same strategies for other workers too.' The rationale behind Justice for Janitors is that organising the contractors alone will not work: the union needs to force building owners to accept the union and accept higher costs so that wages and conditions can improve. As Stephen Lerner, one of the architects of the JforJ strategy put it:

> The problem is that unions will fail if employers correctly believe that signing a contract is committing economic suicide. And that's what happens when we organise one shop at a time: Either we must accept minimal contracts, or we make employers uncompetitive. By targeting industries, and taking wages out of competition, we can rationalise wages and tame market forces. [10]

The contracting arrangements of the janitorial industry, and the high turnover of the workers, meant that SEIU could not rely on National Labour Relations Board campaigns for recognition: building owners would simply switch

---

10. Stephen Lerner, 'Reviving Unions', *Boston Review*.

contractors whenever the union won recognition, and the workforce would change in the time it took to reach an election in the United States.

Success did not come immediately. Initially, SEIU in Washington tried to approach building owners on an amicable basis, asking them to use union contractors. With the exception of a few union-friendly targets such as the headquarters of the different unions in Washington, this led nowhere. There was little incentive for building owners to voluntarily opt to use more expensive union services. SEIU then targeted national companies with mixed union and non-union branches. Pressure was piled on at the unionised branches so that the company agreed to waive the obligation for the non-union branches to go through the long election process, and accepted majority membership as a precondition for bargaining. The major problem remained, however, of how to unionise the quickly growing regional companies in which SEIU had no toehold.

The pivotal moment for SEIU local 82 came in 1996 when the decision was taken to pull the union workers (who had been organised at the national contractors) out on strike. Instead of picketing their own buildings, the workers went to distribute information at buildings using non-union labour. The strike lasted for six months and turned into a justice movement for the non-union janitors. The Justice for Janitors organising model ran along these lines: organisers and activists visited buildings to develop contacts among the non-union janitors. The contacts collected co-workers' addresses, allowing janitors to be visited at home and worker committees to be built up and trained. When there was sufficient worker support, the campaign went public. Through leaflets, visits to the building tenants, and press conferences, tenants and the public were informed about the janitors' working lives: low pay, increasing workload, lack of benefits, occasional non-payment, and building-specific problems - such as the couple who were forced to ride unprotected in an elevator with medical waste. Where this information was not enough to move the tenants to complain to the building owner, JforJ raised hell, demonstrating, doing 'days of noise' outside the building with cymbals and megaphones. The aim was to put such pressure on the building owners that ultimately they would turn around and tell the contractors to accept the union and negotiate for improvements.

The contractors responded by firing large numbers of janitors who were recognised in the demonstrations. But in 1997, the Washington DC commercial janitorial contractors were at last driven into one collective set of negotiations with the union. Finally, in 1998, a master agreement was signed which provided substantial raises and improved benefits. The agreement also had elements that were specifically targeted at the new Latino workforce: it obliged employers to pay 2 cents per worker per hour towards an education centre providing literacy and English language courses.

Local 82 now represents 4000 commercial janitors - 75 per cent of the city's commercial janitors. Naranjo notes that particular effort had to be put into providing the new members with training in the skills required for bargaining and representation, since a number of the workers were from poor rural backgrounds, with minimal or no education. With the major building owners accepting union contractors, and with wages largely removed from inter-contractor competition, there is currently little incentive for the contractors to try to drive the union out: employers seem to have caused few conflicts so far. However, SEIU has not been without problems on how to service janitors who are often part-time workers, and who work in widely dispersed small units. Local 82's solution to the servicing difficulties was to move most of the organisers onto representational work after the collective agreement's settlement, and to create a janitors' drop-in 'help centre' staffed by one union official a day to file grievances.

Meanwhile, the master agreement is due for renewal in 2003, a crucial test for the janitors' organisation. 'If we're going to improve conditions and continue to grow', says Naranjo, 'we can't just say "see you in 2003". Servicing has to be intensive, like organising the union in the first place was. We have to organise and develop new leaders continually.'

Different sector, different tactics: UNITE's Montreal Organising Programme

The Union of Needletrades, Industrial and Textile Employees is the merger of the Amalgamated Clothing and Textile Workers' Union[11] and the International Ladies Garment Workers' Union, unions founded by Jewish clothing workers in 1917 and 1909. As the industrial base has dwindled, hard-hit by the offshoring of production and cheap import penetration, the two unions' combined membership in the United States and Canada has fallen from over a million in

---

11. ACTWU was itself the product of an earlier merger between the Amalgamated Clothing Workers and the Textile Workers Union of America.

the 1970s to a current low of around 250,000.

From the 1970s, the textile and garment unions had undertaken little organising in Canada, and both were profoundly shaken by the 1980s wave of offshoring. The overall Quebec membership had fallen from 29,000 in the mid 1970s to around 5000 in 1996. In 1996, a new organising programme was set up in Montreal. The goal was to organise the world's largest men's suit manufacturer, a factory which employed 2500 Filipino, Chinese, Vietnamese, Latino, Haitian, Bangladeshi, Tamil, Indian and Cambodian workers. UNITE engaged in a two-year fight to push out and replace the factory's company union. Staff were hired from immigrant community and student groups, and volunteer immigrant worker activists were brought in from UNITE factories on both sides of the border. Meetings were held in eight different languages, with translators stationed around the meeting hall. Noisy demonstrations became a fixture on the Montreal evening news, as workers stormed shopping malls, trade shows and - after 47 workers had been fired - their own factory. The campaign was not successful. In 1997, the workers still employed inside the factory, terrified by the firings and by the threat of company closure, voted against UNITE in a company-monitored election over the fate of their in-house union.

UNITE, however, had gained a reputation in Montreal as a union that was willing to fight for immigrants. The organising office was by now a drop-in social centre for immigrant workers, festooned with flags, littered with multi-lingual literature, and packed every day at 4pm when the factories closed. UNITE had also collected a multinational, multilingual organising staff and a body of activists with roots in different immigrant communities. The office became an early port of call for immigrant workers with problems and the organising staff picked up rumours about different factories from their own networks.

UNITE's manufacturing base differs from SEIU's service base in two important respects. First, for most manufacturing there is no longer a possibility of 'taking wages out of competition': manufacturers are competing with goods produced elsewhere. Washington DC will always need janitors, but, even though UNITE has tried to broaden its base from the runaway garment sector, most manufacturing can relocate beyond the union's reach. Second, with the exception of a few high-profile clothing products, there is rarely a public face to manufacturing. The 'consumers' of services go right into the employment area

- tenants' businesses are disrupted when Latino janitors storm elegant office buildings - whereas factories are hidden from view and it is often difficult to create a stir about events in a plastic bottle factory. UNITE therefore usually uses the government-monitored recognition route to form a union in the absence of other ways to pressure an employer into bargaining.

The model used for organising in Montreal begins with setting up clandestine worker committees in different factories and asking worker leaders to collect their co-workers' addresses. On a given date, staff and activists start visiting all the workers from a factory at home, and leaders begin signing up co-workers inside the factory. The aim is to give the employer minimal response time and to reach a majority for legal recognition as fast as possible. Then the union digs in with the workers for the long wait for the official recognition to be issued, followed by negotiations.

UNITE organised 5000 new members in Montreal from 1997 to 1999 - 95 per cent of whom were first generation immigrants - from textile factories, garment factories, food-processing factories, plastic factories and nursing homes. 1500 of these new members came from a sock factory which employed primarily Haitians. Those workers recently won their first collective agreement after a nine month struggle involving demonstrations, work stoppages, and a bitter three week strike during which workers and organisers set up a stereo system and drums outside the factory gates and workers sang and danced daily in the snow, taunting their Italian employers. After the sock factory strike, it became impossible to walk around North-East Montreal without spotting the distinctive black and red UNITE caps. Haitian workers from other workplaces recognised and welcomed UNITE as the union that had struck at the sock factory. There was a widespread and nuanced perception among Haitians that the union had been prepared to stick by the workers, even though the sock factory was still no paradise to work in.

As UNITE began to win contracts for the new members at different workplaces, 'time-off' clauses were negotiated, allowing the recently-organised workers to come out for short periods as volunteer organisers. Non-union workers who met the volunteer activists were assured that they were joining a vibrant workers' movement whose members were committed enough to volunteer their time freely; and the volunteer activists gained new confidence to go back and organise internally in their own shops.

The strength of UNITE's Montreal organising programme lay in its penetration in certain immigrant groups, allowing much-needed rapid growth. However, since UNITE located its organising targets largely through immigrant networks, UNITE ended up much of the time following worker interest rather than an industrial strategy. UNITE in Montreal has recently begun to focus entirely on capital-intensive textiles and on the relatively easy to organise and stable nursing home sector, but the initial organising victories were thinly spread across different sectors, preventing the union from gaining significant bargaining power in any one industry.

A second flaw in the Montreal organising programme was the lack of transition provided for workers between the organising department and the rest of the union. Workers were initially in intensive contact with multi-lingual staff who were available at all times of day and night: upon the signing of the first contract, they moved onto a single, more traditional, less accessible full-time representative. There was a wide gap between the expectations that the members had of their newly formed unions and the measures that the representative was equipped or accustomed to take. The members had continuing urgent problems - the firings, suspensions and disputes over pay systems did not end with the contracts - and the representative (even when she came from the same immigrant group as the new members) was often overwhelmed. The problem was not only with the representatives, but also with the worker leaders who had to readjust to roles as shop stewards as well as fighters, and who had to discover a happy medium between inertia on the one hand and walking out over every grievance on the other. Changes have begun to be made: certain organising staff have been moved into continuing to do representative work after the first collective agreement, and a new project has been set up to provide additional training to activists so that their local branches can be increasingly autonomous.

Acting like a real union

As UNITE and SEIU found, some of the ingredients which determine the success of an immigrant organising programme have to do with establishing an initial link between the union and the workers. In different campaigns, American and Canadian unions have hired immigrant organisers, developed immigrant members as volunteer organisers, put down deep roots in immigrant communities, supported immigrants in their struggles against discrimination and restrictions in the wider society, built coalitions with immigrant organisations, adapted campaign message and campaign tactics to the concerns and strengths of immigrants, and adopted important cultural referents (imagery, songs, priests and prayers on the picket line).

However, for the ties between the union and immigrants to be meaningful and lasting, immigrants also demand that their unions act like real unions – i.e. they support them in the long term in their struggles against their employers. In addition to creative organising methods, immigrants require all the same things from their union as native workers - that they fight for recognition, push for workplace improvements and build viable local branches. In fact, immigrants need standard union gains, benefits and protections more, because their jobs are worse, and these things will be harder to obtain for them because behind most bad jobs are anti-union employers. Unless unions address the deprivations, daily misery, and extreme imbalance of power that make immigrants decide to organise their workplaces, they will be unable to retain their new members or grow in these communities.

The difficulties of organising immigrant workers do not arise from immigrant worker unwillingness to join unions but from the particular jobs they work in, the opposition faced from their employers, and the need for unions to respond adequately to immigrant workers' urgent workplace problems. Ironically, many of the crises experienced in immigrant worker organising programmes come from a failure by unions to fulfil their *traditional* tasks of industrial strategizing, organising, bargaining, representation, and training.

While the level of immigration to the United States and Canada is unusual - foreign born workers are the fastest growing segment of the labour force in both countries - some of the lessons from North American immigrant organising are nonetheless pertinent to unions elsewhere which are in decline and are refocusing upon organising. Unions have choices to make about who they organise: the paradox is that those who most need and want to organise are usually those who require most hard work and struggle to organise into durable unions. If unions accept the challenge of organising workers who, because of age, gender or race are stuck in bad jobs, they will need not only to rethink their strategies but also to rekindle their willingness to struggle and take enormous risks on behalf of their members.

The future of immigrant worker organising in North America is far from clear-cut. For example, despite the encouraging developments described here, the proportion of 'Hispanics' (all those of Latin American origin) who are unionised in the United States continues to fall (only 11.9 per cent of Hispanics are union members [12]). If unions fail to organise and represent the masses of foreign-born workers who are working in the worst jobs the economy has to offer, the prospects for the labour movement and for workers' rights and protections are grim: 'a labor movement that represents a shrinking proportion of the labor force ... will be less able to protect even the interests of the better off strata of the working population. Without adequate economic and political mobilization unorganized workers employed in secondary labor markets ... will suffer. Income polarization ... can be expected to intensify, and ... labor will become more and more divided.' [13]

If, on the other hand, unions are willing to take the risks and pay the costs of fighting for immigrant workers, training immigrant workers, and representing them to the necessary level, then immigrants have the potential to revitalise North American unions and restore some of their original role as a social movement for those who are voiceless at the ballot box. First, however, unions must disabuse themselves of the myths of immigrant worker intractability. As Maria Naranjo of SEIU put it:

A lot of times I hear about seminars on organizing women or third world organizing and I think 'yes, great, there are a lot of technical things you need to know about immigrants, like for example that in Virginia you can't apply for workers' compensation if you are undocumented.' But overall, low wage workers are low wage workers! The most important thing is to understand the industry and to have a good strategy. Throw away the stereotypes when you are organizing immigrants! Like I used to be told that you cannot visit Latino workers at home on Sundays because they are at church. WRONG! You need to compare those stereotypes with the reality of the situation. Like with Salvadoran workers, it is important to understand that they came escaping a war, but you can't because of the war not push them - or they'll never have a union.

---

12. Bureau of Labour Statistics 1998.
13. Robert Asher and Charles Stephenson, *Labor Divided: Race and Ethnicity in United States Labor Struggles 1835-1960*, 1990, p27.

What future for the past in the new South Africa?

David Renton

Dave Renton reflects on what the story of Nongqawuse tells us about modern South African dilemmas.

How should we remember a past which is unpleasant to us? In South Africa, this question is posed by the survival of apartheid-era buildings and monuments. Should they remain intact, or should they be removed? Should the government encourage new memorials to take their place, and if so which events should be commemorated? The history of different regions reveals some of the dilemmas involved. Grahamstown in the Eastern Cape was briefly the second city of the British-ruled Cape province. It was built by English settlers who first arrived in 1820. Promised their own farms by the Imperial British government, the settlers were left to fend for themselves on the arid and inhospitable lands of the region. Within five years, most had returned to the relative comfort of the town. The land was left and turned to weeds and dust, but the city prospered. Traders produced iron goods, wagons and clothes. Museums sprang up, a university, a daily paper, and all the several trappings of civilised life in her majesty's colonies.

Over one hundred and fifty years later, Grahamstown's monuments still reflect the original history of the settlement. The town's camera obscura, a mirror which displays the outside world reflected backwards and upside-down onto a clear white table to form a living panorama of the city, is housed above a typical Grahamstown museum. Towering Victorian patriarchs in top hats address young children, who wear flowery skirts, caps and waistcoats. Beside the models are books authored by Charles Dickens and William Makepeace Thackeray, and old hoardings advertising Coleman's mustard. The images are already fading and dust has begun to settle on the walls. The effect is sobering. For all the undoubted achievements of the town's industrious founders, it is hard to see why they should be remembered now. The patriarchs are dead and their society has crumbled. You might have thought that South Africa could find a new history to complement the transition to democracy and the birth of the new rainbow society, but this new story of the past has yet to be written or agreed.

Elsewhere the images of white Grahamstown's past are less benign. In the place of stuffy patriachs, you find symbols of the country's history of racial exclusion. On the walls of the town's cathedral, it is still possible to trace the marks where the plaques used to hang, indicating which seats were reserved by race. The town guardians have only recently taken down the clips in the church walls, where slaves could be held chained as their masters prayed for redemption. These are not merely the symbols of past inequality. Unemployment in black Grahamstown East stands even now at over 70 per cent. In the townships, basic facilities including water and electricity are absent. Less than half the city's black population registered to vote in the recent general election. Black faces beg today in the town centre, while affluent white citizens walk past.

The new South Africa is to be built on the basis of 'reconciliation'. But does this mean that the awkward details of the past should be forgotten? Is the only hope a future in which all traces of South Africa's history are ignored? This is one message of William Morris's famous utopian novel *News from Nowhere*, in which the hero travels forward in time to discover a utopian future, a Britain freed from the miseries of class and exploitation. In discussion with the narrator, Clara, a happy child of this future socialist society, expresses her disdain for the history books of the past, 'they were well enough for times when intelligent people had but little else in which they could take pleasure, and when they must supplement the sordid miseries of their own lives with imaginations of the lives of other people. [1] For William Morris, one sign of a healthy society would be precisely its lack of interest in history. The houses of Parliament would be used to store manure, while the National Gallery would make little sense when art was equally accessible to all. Once the problems of poverty and oppression were resolved, and mankind had moved on, no-one would need to look back again at the awful events of the past.

In contrast to William Morris, most young South Africans believe that a new history is possible, one which remembers both victories and defeats; but they also recognise that the defeats were shaming and unworthy of pride. I asked Margot, a young black student at Grahamstown's Rhodes University how South Africa constructs its past, 'People in this country don't seem to care about the past, they aren't too bothered by culture. Everything gets divided up. People don't want to know about the history of other groups.' I asked Dave, an older student who had lived in Europe and was more optimistic. 'We've been force-fed a one-sided view of culture for too long. History in this country didn't begin in 1652 or 1820. We've had to review the history books since the change in government. Now we've got to understand the past from both perspectives.' Both wondered if an honest account could be written, yet both also desired to see a history in which all South Africans could share.

I f there is one story which sums up the difficulties in remembering the past of black South Africa, it is the story of the prophetess, Nongqawuse. In Peter Worsley's account, Nongqawuse is the Xhosa equivalent of the millenarian religious leaders of early twentieth century Polynesia, the Tuka in Fiji; or of the champions of the so-called Vailala Madness in Papua New Guinea; each of these movements is described by Worsley in his history of millenarianism, *The Trumpet Shall Sound*. In each of these cases, ordinary people rose up against imperial rule, and used religion to justify their revolt. Their faith in miraculous deliverance led the oppressed to risk everything, sometimes with catastrophic results. [2] Nongqawuse can also be seen as the Xhosa equivalent of the adolescent heroines of European legend, such as Joan of Arc, whose visions helped to liberate France from British rule, or Sophocles's Antigone, who risked her life to give a proper burial to her brother Polyneices. Like Joan of Arc, Nongqawuse

---

1. W. Morris, *News from Nowhere and Other Writings*, Penguin, London (1993 edn), p175.
2. P. Worsley, *The Trumpet Shall Sound*, Paladin, London (1970 edn), pp27-56, 59-84.

became the champion of an entire people; her visions helped to decide the outcome of the wars between the English and the Xhosa. Nongqawuse is one of the most important figures in the history of her country, yet she is largely forgotten in today's South Africa.

The story goes that in March 1856, a 14-year old woman by the name of Nongqawuse claimed to have seen visions, in which she met with ancestors and other long-dead warriors. Her first vision came at the edge of her garden, by the river Gxhara, when two strangers called her over. They entrusted her with a singular message, 'Tell that the whole community will rise from the dead; and that all cattle now living must be slaughtered, for they have been reared by contaminated hands ... There should be no cultivation ... So says the chief Napakade, the descendant of Sifu-sibanzi.' These strangers also announced that they had come from over the waters, from Russia, at whose hands Britain had suffered defeats during the Crimean War. If Nongqawuse obeyed their instructions, then they promised that the British troops would be destroyed as they had been elsewhere.

Nongqawuse told the story of her vision to her uncle, Mhlakaza, a convert to Christianity and a councillor to the Xhosa Chief Sarili. Soon afterwards, he too claimed to see visions, including his long-dead brother. These supernatural warriors told him that if the Xhosa people would kill all their cattle, destroy their stores, and not plant any more grain that year, a whirlwind would come, and blow the English into the sea. Then, their heroes would rise from the dead, bringing with them vast herds of cattle and huge quantities of grain. Not all the councillors believed this message, and indeed several attempted to prevent the sacrifice of the cattle. Yet the situation of the Xhosa was desperate. Under-armed and ill-prepared, they had fought a losing battle against the English settlers for 80 years. The people had already lost the greater part of their land and saw no other means by which they could defeat their better-organised enemy. Peter Worsley suggests that it was this feeling of powerlessness and decay, this sense of despair following the defeats that the Xhosa had suffered, which prompted Chief Sarili and the majority of his people to accept Nongqawuse's word (p238). For whatever reason, the Xhosa set to work. Up to 400,000 cattle were killed and many fields were burned. Nongqawuse's spokesman, her uncle Mhlakaza, predicted that on 8 February 1857, the sun itself would turn round and the skies would be red. Yet on the day itself nothing happened. Soon it became clear that the Xhosa had inflicted upon themselves an extraordinary disaster.

Within a year, the Xhosa population had declined by three-quarters, and up to 40,000 people died. Meanwhile, a similar number fled into the Cape Colony to seek employment with the white population there, as the only means to survive. As the people fled, the governors of the Colony sent troops to harry the survivors. They confiscated the deserted lands, and placed settlers upon them. The survivors were offered charity in the British towns, and when they refused it they were jailed. In the aftermath of tragedy, the English imposed a humiliating military defeat on the starving Xhosa. The Xhosa saw their land taken away from them and their civilisation destroyed. It would be a further fifty years before there were any signs in the black Eastern Cape of a renewed political optimism, with the formation in 1912 of the South African Native National Congress, the parent of today's African National Congress, the ANC.

The interpretation of these events has long been questioned. Not surprisingly, many black South Africans see the tale as a fiction, a distraction from other accounts which concentrate on the more important role of the English colonialists in taking Xhosa land. This cautious attitude is summed up by a Black Consciousness song from the 1970s, 'Sir George Grey took our country/ He entered in through Nongqawuse.' Today's descendants of the Xhosa of the 1850s are right to be cautious of the story of Nongqawuse, for among South Africa's whites, the opposite attitude has prevailed. The history of the cattle killing has been used to demonstrate the necessary and civilising effects of white rule.

Sir George Grey was the English governor of the Colony at the time of the cattle slaughter. He is famous today for his work as a geologist and botanist, and is described in most histories as an enlightened liberal. Grey told his biographer that he had gone to warn the Xhosa against the killing, at 'undue danger' to himself. Yet, in truth, Grey punished those rulers who did not take part in the cull. He also attributed blame for the killing to mischievous chiefs, who had aimed to force their unwilling people into war, through starvation. Meanwhile in Alexandria, where Nongqawuse is buried, her story is used today as evidence of the primitive fanaticism of the 'kaffir'. This opinion is shared even by the white farmers who now own the plots around the land on which Nongqawuse's memorial lies.

Several historians have attempted to provide a history of the cattle slaughter free from the racism and celebration of the original English accounts. Allister Sparks' widely-read *The Mind of South Africa* places the story of Nongqawuse at the end of a succession of defeats, which saw the breaking of the power of the Ndebele and the Zulus, before the Xhosa. In this way, the cattle-killings were 'a last desperate act of resistance': 'The result was a national disaster. Tens of thousands of Xhosa died. Thousands more left their scorched land to stumble starving across the frontier to the white farms looking for work. Xhosa power was broken at last, and another migration into servitude took place.'[3] The advantage of this approach is that it respects the people involved. The dead are treated neither as primitive nor heroic, but they are mourned.

The only full-length study of the movement is by Jeffrey Peires. His moving history of the killings, *The Dead will Arise*, suggests that the cattle-slaughter was a rational, even necessary, response to the arbitrary and cruel nature of British colonialism. The Xhosa had seen their land taken from them, through eight years of colonial wars, and were already suffering from an outbreak of cattle-lung disease, which left 100,000 of their cows dead. In his words, this epidemic 'was a necessary cause of the Xhosa cattle-killing'.[4] In Peires' explanation, the cattle slaughter began as a legitimate, indeed sensible, cull of sick or dying beasts. It spread with the encouragement of the English, often through the intermediary advice of converted Christians among the Xhosa. A central figure was Mhlakaza, Nongqawuse's uncle. It was Mhlakaza who claimed that if the cattle were slaughtered, the dead would rise again. As for the vengeful god Sifu-sibanzi, he had been introduced to the Xhosa by Christian missionaries in the early 1850s, as a mythical figure to represent the life and teachings of Jesus Christ. Sifu-sibanzi was also the hero in the first Xhosa translation of John Bunyan's *Pilgrim's Progress*.

Timothy Stapleton has further examined the roots of the movement, showing that it was the poorest of the Xhosa who took most part, with the poorer chiefs siding with their own starving people. Stapleton describes this

---

3.   A. Sparks, *The Mind of South Africa*, Heinemann, London (1990 edn), pp106-8; also A. Sparks, *Tomorrow is Another Country: the Inside Story of South Africa's Negotiated Revolution*, Heinemann, London 1995.

4.   J. B. Peires, *The Dead Will Arise: Nongqawuse and the Great Xhosa Cattle-Killing Movement of 1856-1857*, Ravan Press, Johannesburg 1989, p124.

affair as a revolutionary war against the British, in which many Xhosa retained a healthy scepticism towards the chiefs and the rulers of their own side. One reason for the 'reluctant sluaghter' by the Xhosas was to undermine an unloved ruling layer of chiefs who owned the greatest number of cows. The problem for the peasant pastoralists was that in waging a war against their own rulers as well as the British, they doomed themselves to defeat. In Tim Stapleton's account, Governor Grey is the chief villain: 'the governor both stimulated and accelerated an uprising against a failed pastoral aristocracy'. [5] It is clear from his work that there is something heroic and tragic about the story of Nongqawuse. Her movement was a failure and its methods were flawed, but the Xhosa did fight, and in their war there was more than a whisper of the victory that has since come.

It says something about the new South Africa that Jeffrey Peires, Nongqawuse's biographer, has become an ANC member of parliament and indeed a junior minister, while Nongqawuse herself is largely forgotten. Two of us visited her memorial this February, and kindly Mrs Fick who owns the land showed us her visitors' book. We were only the fourth group to have seen Nongqawuse's grave all year. Why didn't more people come?, we asked her. Mrs Fick could only say that a civil servant had visited her, and the ministry was in negotiation. Following her directions, we found our way to Nongqawuse's grave. The prophetess's memorial sits on the side of a hill outside the hamlet of Alexandria. Alone in a working cattle field, it is marked only by six trees and a small concealed plaque, which is no larger than a metal card. It took us ten minutes to find the memorial. We knelt for the obligatory photographs, half-ashamed to be acting like tourists where something so awful was remembered.

I spoke to a third student at Rhodes University. Mmeli works as a teacher in the rural Transkei. His pupils are among the very poorest of South Africa's many poor citizens. He is taking a master's degree in Information Technology, so that when in the future there are computers for the schools, there will be someone who can train the teachers to use them. I asked Mmeli why so few people visited Nongqawuse's memorial. 'You have to think yourself into the minds of the people who put it there. They wanted to glorify colonialism and

---

5. T. J. Stapleton, *Maqoma: Xhosa Resistance to the Colonial Advance 1798-1873*, Jonathan Ball Publishers, Johannesburg 1994, pp172-91.

minority rule.' But 40,000 people died. Shouldn't those killed be remembered? 'Yes,' he agreed, 'but nobody is proud of Nongqawuse.' Is there no way to remember events which you are not proud of? 'Maybe there isn't...', he said and paused. Mmeli did not finish the sentence, so I will attempt to finish it myself. Maybe there is no way to celebrate the past when it still hangs over the present. Perhaps there are enough monuments to the dead already. Maybe there cannot be a reconciliation history, while unemployment in Grahamstown East still stands at over 70 per cent. Maybe it is impossible to look back at the history with confidence, when past poverty and past inequality still have such an impact on South Africa today.

If South Africa is to construct a society in which everyone can share, a historical memory must be created which comes to terms with the horrors of the past. Such a history would commemorate the dead of all peoples, while at the same time taking sides. For the dead to be properly remembered, a judgement must be made against the many crimes committed in the name of empire and race, and an honourable role should be assigned to those who took part in the struggle against oppression and racial inequality. This history could only be written as part of a general and thoroughgoing process of reconciliation, broader and also more forward-looking than anything which has been accomplished to date. When such a historical memory is created, one of its first tasks will be to make sense of the sad and disturbing story of the young Xhosa prophetess Nongqawuse.

Mourning the movement

Isaac D. Balbus

Isaac Balbus argues that an inability to mourn the losses of the golden age of the 1960s contributes to our current sense of political pessimism.

Many of us are all still haunted by the ghost of the 1960s. For twenty-five long years we have not ceased either lamenting or celebrating the death of this singular decade. I argue in this essay that the remarkable longevity of this 'Death of the 1960s' story unwittingly testifies to the survival of its subject. For those of us who cut our political teeth on the civil rights, anti-war and student movements, the 1960s live on as a longing for a Golden Age that has been lost to a permanently pallid present. But nostalgia for the 1960s is only the most obvious sign of their ghostly presence. Some commentators are still so spooked by them that they simply cannot refrain from periodically presiding over their burial.[1] The intensity of these efforts to exorcise the 1960s, I would suggest, only serves to confirm the survival of their spirit.

My argument is that this recurrent pattern on the left of both nostalgia for and denigration of the 1960s is at the same time a sign of, and a defence against, a profound political-cultural loss from which we have yet to recover. Both the longing for (an idealised version of) what has been lost and the (seemingly) sober message that nothing valuable was ever really lost ward off the sorrow - and the guilt - that would inevitably accompany a fully embodied awareness of the magnitude of our loss. Both serve, in other words, to defend against the deeply difficult but absolutely indispensable task of mourning (what we used to call) the movement. This task is indispensable because the consequence of evading it, I maintain, is precisely the profound political pessimism from which we presently suffer. We have lived through a transition from a time when - as so many have remarked - everything seemed possible, to a time that seems bereft of any political possibilities at all. I would not want to underestimate the current political-economic reasons for this loss of our radical political imagination. But I also want to insist that our inability to mourn a movement in which the imagination was actually - if only briefly - '*au pouvoir*' is at least as responsible as those 'objective factors' for the current impotence of our imagination.

My argument, in short, is that the atrophy of our imagination is a symptom of our *political depression*.[2] Political depression, I claim, is every bit as much the result of unmourned intersubjective losses as individual depression is the result of unmourned personal losses. In either case hope is crushed under the accumulated weight of unexpressed grief. Thus the renewal of political hope - the resuscitation of our currently moribund political imagination - requires that we summon up the strength for our simultaneously

---

1. Richard J. Ellis, in *The Dark Side of the Left* (University Press of Kansas 1998) contends that the 'illiberalism' or authoritarianism of the New Left was inscribed from the very beginning in its 'radical egalitarian' commitments and that a revitalised progressive movement must therefore abandon those commitments. David Burner complains, in *Making Peace With The Sixties* (Princeton University Press 1996) that the 1960s spawned a divisive 'identity politics' that obscures the common economic interests on which a majoritarian contemporary left movement must be based. In both cases the claim is that nothing of value was lost and thus that the only thing worth learning from the 1960s is how not to repeat them. Frederic Jameson, on the other hand, argues in 'Periodising the 60s', in Sohnya Sayres *et al*, *The 60s Without Apologies* (University of Minnesota Press 1984) that whatever was lost *had to be lost*: 'the 60s had to happen the way [they] did' (p178), as they were but the inevitable effect of 'the transition from one infrastructural or systemic stage of capitalism to another' (p208). Thus for Jameson Historical Necessity recuperates any sense of regret that might otherwise exist. It also dictates that *nothing at all* can be learned from the 1960s: 'nostalgic commemoration of the glories of the 60s or abject confession of the decade's many failures ... are two errors which cannot be avoided by some middle path that threads its way in between (p178). It is precisely 'this middle path' that I attempt to chart in this essay, which should therefore be read as a rejoinder to Jameson's argument.
2. In 1984 the *Social Text* editors of *The 60s Without Apologies* confessed that they found it 'astonishing that the trashing of the 60s in the media generally should be met with so little indignation or resistance ... The numbers of Americans still living today who were involved or touched in at least one political demonstration in the course of the period must be immense. Where are all those people, and what has become of the radical political culture that might normally be expected to emerge from such a tremendous wave of collective experience?' (p8) I believe that the claim that many former 1960s activists are *politically depressed* goes a long way to answering this question and thus explaining the otherwise 'astonishing' absence of 'indignation or resistance'.

emotional and political task of giving in to our grief.

In the next section of this essay I call on the psychoanalysis of Melanie Klein to help us appreciate both the necessity and the difficulty of mourning *individual* losses. The last section summarises the effort of Kleinians and others influenced by her work to extend her model of mourning to political-cultural or intersubjectively shared losses, and concludes with an application of this model of *group mourning* to the specific problem of mourning the movement.

Melanie Klein and the psychoanalysis of individual mourning

It was in fact not Klein but Freud who first supplied the warrant for a psychoanalytic theory of political mourning. 'Mourning', he announces in *Mourning and Melancholia*, 'is regularly the reaction to the loss of a loved person, *or to the loss of some abstraction which has taken the place of one*, such as one's country, an ideal, and so on.'[3] An 'abstraction' takes the place of 'a loved person' in the sense that the libido originally 'invested' in this person is displaced onto that abstraction. Because our ideals serve as substitutes for the people we love, the loss of the former can give rise to 'reactions' of grief that are comparable to the feelings that follow the loss of the latter. Thus the implicit message of Freud's famous definition is that the mourning of cultural or political losses may be as necessary to our emotional well-being as the mourning of the individual losses on which the rest of the essay is explicitly and exclusively focused.

But Freud's model of individual mourning does not satisfy, and in fact is inconsistent with, what I take to be the criteria for an adequate theory of political mourning. His concept of the 'loved person' as the 'cathected object' of the libido of the bereaved prevents him from grasping both the depth and the tenacity of the ties between ourselves and those whom we have lost. Since successful mourning is defined by Freud as a 'detachment of libido' from what has been lost, anything that interferes with eventual 'de-cathexis' is considered to be a sign of melancholia rather than of normal mourning. His text works (although not without some internal inconsistency) to confine ambivalence towards, guilt over, and identification with, the 'lost object' to the category of

---

3. Sigmund Freud, 'Mourning and Melancholia' [1917], *The Standard Edition of the Complete Psychological Works* (hereinafter cited as SE) vol.14, Hogarth Press, London 1957, p243.

the pathological.[4] Thus it can not serve as the foundation for the theory of political mourning that it authorises.

But Klein's text can. All the features of mourning that are marginalised in Freud's 'Mourning and Melancholia' become central to Melanie Klein's concept of mourning in her 'Mourning and its Relation to Manic-Depressive States'.[5] Unlike Freud, Klein plumbs the emotional depths of the relationship between the mourner and the love (s)he has lost. Freud was aware, of course, that every person repeats their relationship with their parents in the course of their ostensibly adult relationships. But it was left to Klein to grasp the meaning of this repetition for mourning. Beneath the loss of the adult other, she argues, there always lurks the threatened loss of the (internal) mother: 'the poignancy of the actual loss of a loved person is ... greatly increased by the mourner's unconscious phantasies of having lost his *internal* "good" objects as well' ('Mourning', p353). This is why, according to Klein, mourning is typically both so painful and prolonged: 'early mourning is revived whenever grief is experienced in later life' ('Mourning', p344) .

By 'early mourning' Klein means the 'anxieties, guilt and feelings of loss and grief derived from the depressive position' ('Mourning', p 353) - i.e., the turbulent emotional atmosphere surrounding the very young child's separation from the mother. She argues that the adult mourner will choke in this atmosphere if the child never learned how to breathe in it. Learning to breathe in the depressive position, moreover, is no easy matter for the young child. Because the mother is the source of both the satisfaction and the frustration of the imperious needs of the infant, Klein argues that the infant necessarily phantasises both a 'good mother' (actually she says 'breast') who is the source of all pleasure and a 'bad mother' who is the source of all pain. The 'good mother' thus becomes the object of the child's love and the 'bad mother' becomes the target for his/her rage. Successfully negotiating the depressive position requires that the child 'work

---

4. *Ibid., passim.* In Freud's later writings this clear-cut opposition between mourning and melancholia is implicitly called into question, especially in *The Ego and The Id* , where the ego is defined as 'a precipitate of abandoned object-cathexes'; i.e., identification with the 'lost object' is constitutive of the sense of self (*The Ego and the Id* [1923], SE vol.19, p29). But Freud never re-theorises mourning in the light of this effort to modify his drive theory.

5. Melanie Klein, 'Mourning and its Relation to Manic-Depressive States', in *Love, Guilt and Reparations and Other Works*, The Free Press, New York 1984 (hereafter referred to as 'Mourning').

through' and eventually overcome this split between love for the all-good mother and hate for the all-bad mother. But this integration of the good and bad mother is invariably threatened by the profound anxiety and guilt that accompanies the child's dawning awareness that s/he has destroyed - in phantasy, but for the very young child there is of course no difference between phantasy and reality - that very mother whom s/he loves and on whom s/he so deeply depends. The anxiety and guilt will ordinarily awaken in the child an impulse to make reparations to the mother which - if made and accepted - will eventually enable child to discover that the mother has survived his/her rage. Thus, if all goes well, depressive anxiety and guilt are self-limiting, and do not prevent depressive integration. But all may not go well, because the child is always vulnerable to the temptation to defend against anxiety and guilt either by denying that s/he depends on the mother ('manic denial') or by denying that s/he hates her ('idealisation'). These defences interrupt the integration of love and hate on which the emotional development of the child depends. [6] (In *Marxism and Domination* and 'De-Kleining Feminist Mothering Theory?', among other earlier works, I argued - following Dorothy Dinnerstein in *The Mermaid and the Minotaur* (Harper & Row 1976) - that the 'mother-monopolized' *structure* of early child-care itself militates against the successful negotiation of the depressive position, and that it must, therefore, be replaced by co-parenting. I continue to believe that this is the case. But if co-parenting is *necessary*, it is *not sufficient*, for depressive integration. Winnicott is helpful in identifying the (co-parenting) *practices* that would facilitate this integration. For the beginnings of a synthesis of a feminist psychoanalytic focus on child-rearing structures and an object-relational focus on child-rearing practices, see my *Emotional Rescue: The Theory and Practice of a Feminist Father* (Routledge 1998), especially chapter 12.)

Winnicott adds that defensive temptations will be irresistible if the actual mother is not 'good enough', that is, if the mother does not encourage her child's reparative impulses and thus enable the child to alleviate her\his own anxiety and guilt. A mother who is generally able both to encourage her child's flights from the nest and to welcome her\him back to the nest when (s)he falters will engender more love, and less hate, than a mother who normally either suppresses any separation or prematurely pushes the child

6. See D.W. Winnicott, *The Maturational Processes and the Facilitating Environment* (Hogarth Press1965); and *Through Pediatrics to Psychoanalysis* (Hogarth Press 1975).

away. And the more favourable the ratio of love to hate, the stronger the reparative inclinations of the child are likely to be. But even the most supportive mother will - indeed should - frustrate the demands of her child and will therefore become the object of the child's rage. The way in which the mother responds to this rage also affects the intensity of the child's depressive anxiety and guilt. An actual mother who calmly withstands her child's rage is far more likely to foster an internal representation of a caring mother who has survived the child's destructiveness than a mother who either retaliates or 'falls to pieces' in the face of that rage. The reality of 'good-enough' mothering is thus the most important single contribution to the creation of an internal representation of a 'good-enough' mother on which the successful negotiation of the depressive position depends.

According to Klein's argument, the successful negotiation of the depressive position is, in turn, the key to successful mourning as an adult. As Winnicott summarises:

> If in an individual the depressive position has been achieved and fully established, then the reaction to loss is grief, or sadness. Where there is some degree of failure at the depressive position the result of loss is depression (*Through Paediatrics*, p275).

Since the separation from the loved-one reproduces the separation from the mother, the bereaved cannot but hate the 'object' for having 'abandoned' her/him and cannot but feel guilty for hating the object (s)he also loves. This guilt is only compounded by the phantasy that the hatred that (s)he sometimes felt for the loved-one while he or she was alive was somehow responsible for his or her death ('Mourning', p352-5). If the bereaved adult never learned as a child how to respond reparatively to depressive guilt - if (s)he has no confidence that love can triumph over hate - then (s)he will succumb to the temptation to defend against it either by denying her love or by denying her hate. The former entails a (manic) 'denial of the meaningfulness of the loss' and the latter entails a 'persistent [idealised] attachment to the lost object'.[7] Either form of denial

---

7. Max Forman, 'Two Defenses Against the Work of Mourning', in Sol Altschul (ed), *Childhood Bereavement and its Aftermath* (International Universities Press 1988), p378. See also Hans W. Loewald, 'Internalization, Separation, Mourning, and the Superego', *The Psychoanalytic Quarterly*, vol.3 1962, especially pp485-87.

will transform mourning into melancholia. Conversely, this pathological outcome can only be avoided if the mourner has the emotional wherewithal simultaneously to acknowledge both her hatred and her love for the lost object. Making room for her rage will engage the reparative impulses of the 'depressively integrated' mourner and will eventually enable her to experience 'in full force … the pining for the lost object' ('Mourning', p360).

This excruciating experience is essential for the completion of the mourning process:

[When] grief is experienced to the full and despair is at its height, the love for the object wells up and the mourner feels more strongly that life … will go on after all, *and that the lost love object can be preserved* within ('Mourning', p360).

Thus for Klein the successful work of mourning culminates in a certain kind of *identification* with the lost object. We can infer from her insistence on the mourner's need to recognise and work through his ambivalence toward the lost object that this identification must be *selective* in the sense that only positive attributes of the object are taken in by, and become part of the self, while others are left behind. What is implicit in Klein is made explicit by subsequent theorists of mourning who have been influenced by her account:

[A] successful resolution of the grief process depends on a … healing identification with valued aspects of the deceased person. The uncomplicated mourner is able to discriminate realistically among the traits of the deceased and identify those he values positively … In contrast the depressed mourner experiences a *disruptive* identification with ambivalently related representations of the deceased that eventuates in a continuing internal struggle - a struggle between cherishing the self and wanting to do away with it.[8]

Identifications for purposes of growth are not imperative, emergency, 'in toto' internalisations. The various aspects of the objects can be

---

8.   Vamik Volkan, *Linking Objects and Linking Phenomena*, International Universities Press 1981, pp13-14,112-3.

experienced and specific ones can be relinquished or co-ordinated as enduring aspects of the self. The difference is between relatively enforced and relatively optional identifications. The latter tend to be with the loved and admired traits of the object.[9]

Klein claims that these selectively loving identifications with the lost object often result in the enhanced 'productive activity' of the bereaved:

At this stage in mourning, suffering can become productive ... [It can] stimulate sublimations, or even bring out quite new gifts in some people, who may take to painting, writing, or other productive activities ... Others become more productive in a different way - more capable of appreciating people and things, more tolerant in their relations with others - they become wiser ('Mourning', p360).

Thus we can say that for Klein (successful) mourning is a process in which *grief transforms loss into growth*. But she also insists that this must happen twice if it is to happen even once. As we have seen, the loss of the adult other necessarily threatens the loss of the (adult) child's (internal) mother. Any current loss will confront even the most securely 'depressively integrated' adult with the task of 'reinstating ... his loved *internal* objects [which] are felt to have gone under' ('Mourning', pp362,353). According to Klein, 'the successful work of mourning' requires the 'rebuilding of this inner world' (p363). Thus the selective identification of the bereaved with his currently lost other on which his development depends is contingent on the reconstruction of his identification with his long-lost mother. Klein's ultimate message, then, is that grief can only transform current loss into growth by '*recovering* what ... has already [been] attained in childhood' (p362). Only by rescuing his past does the mourner give her/himself a future.

Conclusion: mourning the movement mother

If we assume, with Freud, that *ideals take the place of the loved-one*, and with Klein, that *the loved-one is ultimately the mother*, then it follows that the account

---

9. Joseph H. Smith, 'On the Work of Mourning', in B. Schoenberg, *et. al., Bereavement: Its Psychological Aspects*, Columbia University Press 1975, p20.

of individual mourning I have outlined can also serve as the skeleton for my account of mourning the movement. In order to flesh out this account, however, I need to say something more specific about the way in which counter-cultural 'ideals' have 'taken the place' of 'the loved-one', that is, about the precise sense in which *the movement was a mother* to its youthful members.

Contemporary Kleinians have extended Klein's analysis of the relationship between the child and his/her mother to the relationship between the individual and his group.[10] They assume that groups are unconsciously experienced as simultaneously gratifying and frustrating mothers that inevitably evoke both the gratitude and the rage of their members. Thus the group that is loved is also necessarily the group that is hated. The development of the group demands that its members learn to respond reparatively to the anxiety and the guilt aroused by this ambivalence; that is, that they come to understand that their group is neither all-good nor all-bad but nonetheless worthy of care. But this happy outcome is always threatened by the temptation to defend against the group equivalent of depressive anxiety and guilt, either by denying one's dependence on the group (the group analogue of manic denial) or by denying one's rage against it (the group analogue of idealisation). Manic denial leads to dropping out of the group but includes an obsessive preoccupation with, and denigration of, the very group from which one has dropped out. Idealisation creates a demonised out-group that unwittingly becomes the target for all the rage that cannot be expressed within the in-group. Thus the Kleinian message is that the development of the group (as well as the development of its individual members) depends on the capacity of its members to acknowledge and work through, rather than defend against, the ambivalence and guilt that inevitably accompany membership in the group. Group development is possible but precarious.

It seems to me that this general account does much to illuminate the specific psycho-dynamics of the 1960s. In the light of that account it makes sense to say, to begin with, that the movement was a particularly gratifying mother. Its pervasive presence protected us from the dangers of an often hostile outside world and gave us a feeling of belonging to something much larger

---

10. For a useful summary of this literature, see C. Fred Alford, *Melanie Klein and Critical Social Theory*, Yale University Press 1989, chapter 3.

than ourselves. Through our common identification with our movement mother, we who would have otherwise encountered each other as strangers immediately became 'brothers' and 'sisters' with whom food, dope or shelter could be shared. That the language of kinship was regularly employed to express the ties that bound people to one another itself testifies to the maternal origins of the sense of, and need for, *community* that ran so deep during the 1960s. The words of one activist help us recall just how deeply we desired it: 'you've got to build community above all else ... I never had it until I [joined the movement] and I haven't been able to live without it since'.[11] *I haven't been able to live without it since.* For this movement activist, as well as many others, to be separated from the 'beloved community' was to be separated from the source of life itself. But within the matrix of the movement we were safe from what Sartre called the stultifying 'seriality' of modern industrial society. Thus the movement was, in Sartre's sense, a gigantic 'group-in-fusion' in which 'each [member] saw in the Other the same project as his own [and] impersonality, isolation [and] atomisation were washed away'.[12]

The movement on which we so deeply depended, moreover, was also the movement that encouraged us to 'do our thing'. Like Winnicott's 'good-enough-mother' it 'mirrored' us even as it 'held' us: it applauded the widest - often the wildest - possible use of our imagination and thereby bolstered our confidence in our capacity to act creatively in and on the world. Just as the child mirrored by its mother 'not only plays at being a grocer or a teacher, but also at being a windmill or a train'[13] so the youthful members of the movement mobilised (what Walter Benjamin would call) their 'mimetic faculties' simultaneously to find and create all kinds of connections among all manner of ostensibly separate material things. This qualitatively different sense of space, moreover, was

---

11. Edward P. Morgan, *The Sixties Experience: Hard Lessons About Modern America*, Temple University Press 1991, p10. The fact that so many new left activists were so intensely mother-identified also testifies to the maternal origins of their identification with the movement. See Isaac D. Balbus, *Marxism and Domination* Princeton University Press 1982, pp391-94.

12. Mark Poster, *Existential Marxism in Postwar France*, Princeton University Press 1975, p288.

13. Walter Benjamin, 'Doctrine of the Similar', *New German Critique*, no.17 spring 1979, p65.

accompanied by a radically transformed sense of time. For those of us who inhabited this radically re-enchanted world, Benjamin's *Jetztzeit* - the magical time of the Now - became more real than the 'homogeneous, empty time'[14] of modernity which we rejected when we threw away our watches. In short, we were no longer merely 'marking time' but were actually (or so we thought) *making history.* This perhaps unparalleled sense of collective agency gave clear and compelling purpose to our daily lives. Small wonder that for so many of us the 1960s survive as the memory of an Eden from which we were long ago exiled.

But we have many painful memories of that period as well. The movement was no exception to the general rule that even the most gratifying group inevitably frustrates the needs of its individual members. Our patience for participatory democracy was tested, and in many cases worn thin, by the seemingly endless movement meetings that devoured so much of our time. Longstanding personal and professional dreams were deferred, and in some cases permanently sacrificed, to the demands of political activism. The movement's message that 'if you can't be with the one you love [you should] love the one you're with' took a terrible toll on the personal lives of many of its members. In short, the protection and the 'mirroring' of the movement was often purchased at the high price of its intolerance for many of the values to which many of us were still at least ambivalently committed.

That the movement was a *counter*-cultural movement compounded the personal pain that it provoked. To be a member of the movement we had to cut many of our ties to the 'straight society' to which it was opposed. Since membership in the movement was in large part generationally defined, moreover, cutting our ties to that society very often meant cutting ourselves off from our *parents.* Thus many of the children of the movement lost the support of the culture and the families that had given birth to them. But I do not remember a single movement meeting at which these terrible losses were discussed. It was if lamenting those losses would have been a sign of disloyalty to our newly adopted, jealous, movement mother.

I believe that the inability to grieve these losses had grievous consequences. *The very things that we lost became targets for the rage that could not be expressed*

---

14. Benjamin, 'Theses on the Philosophy of History', in Hannah Arendt, *Illuminations,* Schocken Books 1969, p261.

against the movement that was, in part, responsible for our losing them. The defence against our ambivalence took the form of an idealisation of our adopted movement mother and a demonisation of the cultural and biological 'parents' against which we protested. We transformed cops into 'pigs' and re-wrote 'America' with a 'k' as a sign of our struggle against a 'fascism' from which we believed we were entirely free. Our warning that no one over thirty should be trusted was an implicit proclamation that we were completely trustworthy. Why should we who were so 'good' have to lament the loss of 'they' who were so 'bad'?

Of course 'they' all-too-often acted like the 'bad mothers' we took them to be. The actual hostility of both the state and our parents confirmed our paranoid projections and further fuelled our rage against 'the system'. This only led, of course, to still more repression. And so on. Eventually the loving counter-cultural community was lost to this vicious cycle of schizoid opposition between the movement and the system. 'Burned out' or afraid of being 'rubbed out', we left in droves the movement that we loved. We have been politically depressed ever since.

At the outset of this essay I suggested that this depression will not lift until we are finally able to mourn the movement. Now it should be clear what mourning the movement would mean. It would mean doing *now* what we were unable to do *then*: acknowledging and working though our intense ambivalence toward our counter-cultural movement mother. It would require that we 'own' the anger against it that we did not have the strength to express when we first felt it and which we split-off with such fateful consequences. It would also require that we confront our buried guilt both for hating the movement we loved and then for leaving it because we spoiled it with our split-off hate. Facing our anger and our guilt should engage our reparative impulses and remind us just how much we still love what we have lost. Then grief could be 'experienced to the full' and the 'lost loved-object' could be 'preserved within'; i.e. mourning the movement might culminate in a *selective identification* with those (loving) aspects of the 1960s that are truly worth saving. If Klein is correct, this selective identification with the 1960s should 'stimulate [the] productive activity' of our political imagination and even encourage us once again to 'take our dreams for reality'. Thus through a 'regretful sorrow' might we win back our 'devotion to happiness which has been denied'.[15]

This sorrow, finally, will have to find both public and private expression. From Klein we have learned that our 'real' adult losses awaken early childhood losses and that our capacity to mourn the former will in important part be determined by our capacity to mourn the latter. If we have not learned to tolerate our ambivalence for our 'internal objects', we will not be in an emotional position to tolerate our ambivalence for the 1960s. Thus the individual struggles of so many 68-ers both inside and outside therapy to mourn their internal mothers (and fathers) are a necessary complement to the shared mourning of the movement on which, I have argued, their development equally depends.

It was precisely a commitment to the movement that motivated many of us to begin long ago the individual grief-work that has since become necessary for the successful mourning of that very movement. Those of us who were committed to the principle that we should live our lives as if the good society already existed were soon forced to face the fact that the only way in which we could live up to this principle was to do compensatory emotional work on our selves. We recognised that a 'prefigurative politics'[16] required a personal transformation: there could be no successful struggle against the domination in our society without a successful struggle against the domination within *us*. I believe that many of us are now far more emotionally prepared for prefigurative politics than we were thirty years ago: we have caught up psychologically with our political commitment to combat domination. But ironically the very political task for which we are now emotionally prepared seems virtually unimaginable.

This loss of political imagination, I have argued in this essay, is the result of a collective failure to mourn a movement that gave birth to a profound and pervasive sense of social solidarity and collective agency. All the individual grief-work in the world will not help us to work through the terrible loss of that sense of solidarity and collective agency we have suffered, and for which we are, in part, responsible. Social losses - intersubjectively shared losses - can only be properly mourned in a properly social setting.[17] Thus ongoing

---

15. Theodor W. Adorno, *Prisms*, Neville Spearman 1967, p230.
16. Wini Breines, *Community and Organization in the New Left, 1962-68*, Praeger 1982, pp1-8.
17. Eric L. Santner, *Stranded Objects*, Cornell University Press, 1990, pp53,126-7,147; Kenneth J. Doka, *Disenfranchised Grief: Recognizing Hidden Sorrow*, Lexington Books 1989, pp80,86-7,133,330.

individual grief-work is a necessary complement to, but is no substitute for, the collective grief-work that we have yet to accomplish; mourning the movement and reclaiming our childhood are two equally essential, reciprocally related, routes to that 'hope in the past'[18] that would reanimate our petrified present. Personal and political grief work are, in short, two sides of the same emancipatory coin. The same coin, but two different sides. The personal both *is* and *is not* the political. This is, it seems to me, one of the hard-won, enduring insights that must be saved from the 1960s.

---

18. Benjamin, 'Theses on the Philosophy of History', p255.

Anti-Fascist Action

Radical resistance or rent-a-mob?

Mark Hayes and Paul Aylward

Mark Hayes and Paul Aylward analyse the nature of Anti-Fascist Action.

There appears to be a general consensus amongst political commentators that there is a re-emerging fascist threat in contemporary Europe. As Roger Eatwell has noted,

> waves of extreme and radical right-wing activity have been washing up over European shores during the half-century since the total military defeat of Fascism. Yet, until recently, the long-term electoral prospects of such parties have appeared minimal ... but as the new millennium beckons, the latest western European wave appears to be the most threatening one for fifty years.[1]

The re-emergence of the fascist spectre has been graphically reflected in the political prominence of Le Pen's *Front National* in France, and in the success of Jorg Haider and the Freedom Party in Austria. Moreover, with unemployment

---

1. R. Eatwell, 'The Dynamics of Right-Wing Electoral Breakthrough', *Patterns of Prejudice*, Vol 32 No 3, July 1998, p3.

in Europe standing at over 30 million, and economic crisis threatening to undermine political stability across the region, there is growing concern that fascist ideas will once again begin to resonate. As Chantal Mouffe has pointed out, the resurgence of the extreme right should be seen in the context of a 'bland homogenised political world', where 'the left' has, in essence, capitulated to neo-liberal hegemony, and where ideological convergence allows the more extreme populist parties on the right to portray themselves as the 'radical' alternative to the dominant consensus'.[2] With the left out-manoeuvred in ideological terms, and in the absence of genuine political choice, it is not difficult to envisage widespread disaffection in society, and this might well provide practical political opportunities for the far right.

However, whilst we acknowledge the dangers inherent in the contemporary situation, the fact is that fascist organisations in Britain have, as yet, singularly failed to make any significant political or electoral impact. There have been various explanations for this, some more plausible than others.[3] For instance, there has sometimes been an assumption (albeit implicit in some cases) that the indigenous population has been, or is, characterised by the extent to which it has imbued 'liberal' values. So from this perspective the primary reason for fascism's failure to take root has been/is the pervasive tolerance and forbearance of the British population. This approach, although comforting, is clearly inadequate, and other factors have undoubtedly had a more significant effect. For instance, it is undoubtedly the case that Britain has not experienced the kind of severe economic and social crisis which might have precipitated widespread discontent with liberal democratic forms and structures. Socio-economic dislocation in Britain has been regionalised and sporadic. It is also evident that the fascist groups themselves have been persistently undermined in their efforts by their own political and organisational

---

2. See C. Mouffe, 'The Radical Centre: A Politics Without Adversary', *Soundings*, Issue No 9 Summer 1998. There are many useful accounts of fascism and fascist ideology; see, for example, R. Griffin, *The Nature of Fascism*, Routledge 1993; M. Kitchen, *Fascism*, Macmillan 1976; R. Eatwell, *Fascism: A History*, Chatto and Windus 1995; and W. Laqueur (ed), *Fascism: A Reader's Guide*, Pelican 1982.
3. See M. Cronin (ed), *The Failure of British Fascism*, Macmillan 1996; and R. Thurlow, *Fascism in Britain*, I. B. Tauris 1998; and R. Thurlow, 'The Failure of British Fascism' in A. Thorpe (ed), *The Failure of Political Extremism in Inter-War Britain*, University of Exeter 1989.

ineptitude. Moreover, the existence of a conventional constitutional right-wing Conservative Party has inevitably undermined support for potential populist alternatives; and the absence of any credible left-wing (Communist) threat has meant that fascists have not been able to exploit the fear that this might have generated. In any case, the mechanics of the electoral system in Britain tend to make it extremely difficult for smaller parties to make a significant impact. In addition to all of this, the fascist groups have never been able (or indeed in some cases willing) to overcome the negative historical legacy of the second world war and, more specifically, the Holocaust. Naturally, this experience has been enough to convince most rational people that fascism (particularly the Nazi version) was a grotesque and irredeemable political creed.

So, for a variety of inter-related reasons (some of which are more plausible than others), fascism in Britain has never really prospered politically. Of course the fact that the British Union of Fascists, the National Front or the British National Party have failed to make significant political headway should not lead to complacency. It would be a mistake to accept uncritically the notion of British exceptionalism, and even whilst operating at the margins of politics such organisations have the capacity to inflict serious damage upon the social fabric.

Given the evident threat posed by the extreme right, fascist groups and parties have always inadvertently managed to precipitate the formation of anti-fascist organisations - groups specifically designed for the purpose of eradicating the fascist threat. In the contemporary context perhaps the most well known (and certainly the most vocal) of these groups has been the Anti-Nazi League. The ANL was founded in November 1977 in response to the perception that the NF had achieved a measure of electoral success, especially in London. In fact the NF's vote was largely the result of differential turnout in local elections, but the tactic of 'controlling the streets' in order to 'march and grow', which was articulated by the likes of Martin Webster (NF National Activities Organiser), was always likely to induce opposition. Although the nucleus of the ANL was provided by the Trotskyist Socialist Workers' Party, it was successful in attracting support from the wider labour and trade union movement. It was also able to achieve a prominent media profile through cultural activities such as 'Rock Against Racism'. In many respects therefore it could be argued that the ANL provided the paradigm for other similar groups which emerged subsequently, such as 'Youth Against Racism in Europe' and the

'Anti-Racist Alliance' (indeed the ANL itself was re-launched in 1992). However, there is one particular anti-fascist organisation that has sought to set itself apart and which, in terms of media exposure and academic analysis, has been significantly under-researched. This is 'Anti-Fascist Action'.

Anti-Fascist Action was originally set up in 1985 and attempted to differentiate itself from other similar groups by the extent to which it was willing to advocate the use of violence in pursuit of overriding objectives. This has led to criticism of AFA as, among other things, an organisation engaged in the 'politics of the punch up', 'macho posturing', 'squadism' and even 'terrorism'. Indeed the conventional perception was probably best expressed by Peter Paterson when he described AFA as 'a group which looks suspiciously like left-wing Fascists eager for a street war with right-wing Fascists' (Daily Mail 19.5.92). In fact extensive primary research recently conducted would tend to suggest that such criticisms tend to oversimplify a relatively sophisticated political phenomenon. [4]

AFA was formed principally by disgruntled members of the ANL, who coalesced around the 'no platform for Fascists' strategy. AFA activists felt that, given the BNP's tactical predisposition for street confrontations as a means of attracting white working-class support, a commitment to physical resistance was a prerequisite for effective anti-fascism. Fascists would thereby be confronted by a clear physical as well as ideological opposition. Underpinning this approach was a pervasive scepticism about the utility of purely legal methods, and a belief that an over-reliance on the state might well precipitate legislation which could be deployed against 'extremists' on the left as well as the right (as the Public Order Act was utilised after 1936). Moreover, AFA activists maintained that there had always been a strong tradition of physical force anti-fascism in Britain, which could be traced back through the 62 Group, the 43 Group, the 'battle of Cable Street' and indeed to British members of the International Brigades who fought in Spain in the 1930s. AFA would claim to be the legitimate inheritors of this tradition.

The objective of AFA was unambiguous - to cause maximum disruption to

4. See P. Aylward and M. Hayes: 'Anti-Fascist Action: An Ethnographic Investigation into an Organisation on the Periphery of Politics', paper presented to PSA (Politics of Law and Order Group) 14 November 1998. The paper was based on research which included extensive interviews and participant observation.

fascist activities by whatever means necessary. AFA took seriously Adolph Hitler's observation in *Mein Kampf* that 'only one thing could have stopped our movement - if our adversaries had understood its principle and, from the first day, had smashed with the utmost brutality the nucleus of our new movement'.

As far as AFA was concerned they would tolerate no more meetings, marches or paper sales; as Martell put it, 'only when they [fascists] are too terrified to work in the estates and walk the streets can anti-Fascists be satisfied'. [5]

'AFA would claim to be the inheritors of the British tradition of physical force anti-fascism'

Organisationally, AFA was formed on a regional basis across England, Wales and Scotland. There were four regions and thirty-six branches, which operated autonomously under the auspices of the head office in London. Although AFA does not release detailed membership figures, particular areas of strength included London, Birmingham, Manchester and Glasgow. The original organisers believed that a non-sectarian approach was essential in ensuring that energy was not wasted in engaging in conflict over esoteric points of political theory. Antagonism toward fascism superseded everything, and this single-issue agenda enabled activists from groups like Class War, Direct Action Movement and Red Action to collaborate at an operational level. Anarchists, Trotskyists and radicals of all description were enjoined to enter the fray against the 'common enemy'.

It is certainly the case that at the operational level AFA is far more flexible and sophisticated than the conventional 'rent-a-mob' interpretation would suggest. AFA has sought to make an impact in various ways. For example, as well as playing an active role in 'Unity' carnivals, AFA has attempted to influence the youth music scene through, for example, ventures like 'Cable Street Beat' (formed 1988) and 'Freedom of Movement' (formed 1995). AFA has also attempted to disengage football supporters from fascist influence via various fanzines such as *Red Attitude* (Manchester United), *Well Prepared* (Aston Villa) and *Tiocfaidh Ar La* (Glasgow Celtic). AFA also produces a magazine *Fighting Talk*, launched in 1991, which provides an outlet for theoretical articles, information and news. Indeed international contacts have also been fostered

---

5. S. Martell, 'The Nature of the Beast', *Fighting Talk*, Issue No14, July 1996, p14.

in an attempt to manufacture multilateral collaboration, and to forestall any attempt to marginalise and criminalise militant anti-fascism. (In October 1997 a conference was organised with delegates from Germany, USA, Sweden, Denmark, Holland, Ireland, France, Spain and Canada). Activity is thus conducted in a number of areas in order to articulate an ideological response to fascism.

Even when it comes down to the specifics of street confrontation the AFA 'mobilisations' are relatively well organised and disciplined (see 'Anti-Fascist Action' ((footnote 4). 'Contact' with 'the enemy' is invariably preceded by extensive intelligence gathering and 'scouting'. Objectives are clearly defined and relayed through the so-called 'stewards group'; and in order to minimise difficulties in the event of arrest literature is distributed beforehand which deals with police interrogation techniques and legal procedure. In adopting its abrasive approach AFA has had, given its own stated objectives, some notable 'successes'. The most significant of these 'successes' was arguably the 'set piece' confrontation which took place at Waterloo station in October 1992, which abruptly ended 'Blood and Honour's' attempt to organise openly. ('Blood and Honour' was the organisation set up to control and exploit the lucrative, if largely clandestine, Nazi music scene.) At one level this incident has assumed the status of a 'cultural icon' for AFA members, since 'Waterloo 92' has become an emblem of AFA's capacity to confront and defeat fascism at street level.

Certainly AFA members are absolutely clear on the utility of violence in opposing fascist activity. As one prominent AFA activist put it

> ...they [BNP] can work a local area, going on about local issues, and build up a nice swathe of support, a kind of comfort zone ... and then we could meet them on the streets and in a twenty minute period all that work is gone in one clash, because they'd be outflanked by a more ruthless element and the damage that does them is immeasurable, couldn't be quantified, you couldn't imagine the damage inflicted, not just physically but emotionally and psychologically, logistically and strategically (Interview 'G', in 'Anti-Fascist Action', see note 4).

Indeed it is a little known fact that the organisation Combat 18 was set up in 1992 specifically as a response to the activities of AFA, and in an attempt to protect those activists engaged in the BNP's 'Rights for Whites' campaign in east London.[6]

It is important to note that underlying AFA's approach is not a moralistic antagonism to fascism, although undoubtedly there is an element of this, particularly in terms of individual motivations. The strategy was based upon a considered analysis which stressed the political orientation of fascism as reactionary, ultra-Conservative and anti-working class. It reflected a belief that any effective resistance had to be constructed around the working-class communities which stood to suffer if fascism was successful, but which, paradoxically, formed part of the potential constituency for any burgeoning fascist movement. This orientation towards and within the working class has become particularly important given recent events and the change in strategy of the BNP.

The BNP in April 1994 made a conscious decision to eschew the politics of street confrontation in favour of a Euro-Nationalist strategy which prioritises success via the ballot box. BNP strategists began to work on the reasonable assumption that the general public was unlikely to support a party which had a predisposition for violence carried out by racist bigots. As the BNP put it 'no more marches, meetings, punch-ups ...'; moreover, as a key BNP leader explained,

> the reason for abandoning confrontational street politics was because it hindered our political progress, and was the only thing holding our extreme opponents together ... not that such brawls were of the party's making, but the party invariably got the blame ... and it harmed us politically. Which is primarily why the party has left that sorry excuse for politics behind for good.[7]

This strategic re-orientation did, however, induce some immediate difficulties. There ensued an acrimonious split between the main body of the BNP and the more pro-active hard-core Nazis grouped around Combat 18, many of whom threw in their lot with the so-called 'National Socialist Alliance'. It is perhaps important to note at this juncture that C18 was always prone to internal disputes

---

6. See C. Sargent, quoted in *Independent on Sunday*, 1 February 1998. In fact AFA received a letter bomb in early 1997 from Danish Fascists with links to C18.
7. *Spearhead*, April 1994; T. Lecomber, 'Red Force: Spent Force of Reaction', *Spearhead*, December 1997.

and was eventually incapacitated by extensive state infiltration. Despite the sometimes hysterical reaction of the media, this semi-clandestine hooligan outfit never really posed a serious political threat (indeed its potential to do damage to the social fabric was sometimes overstated by certain anti-fascist organisations, which had a perverse self-interest in exaggerating its importance).

The BNP is a qualitatively different matter. With the socialist left in turmoil and the Labour Party staking out its ideological terrain on ground previously occupied by Thatcherite Conservatives, the BNP hopes to exploit the desire for a radical alternative within the disillusioned (and effectively disenfranchised) white working class. As the BNP's Tony Lecomber put it:

> ... the BNP will almost certainly make its next breakthrough in a run-down working-class area. The people who have been abandoned by Labour and who have never been represented by the Tories will, in their desperation, turn to us ... We are the radical opposition; we speak for the put-upon working class and increasingly for the middle class as well; we set the agenda. We are the future ... ('Red Force', see note7)

By overtly and explicitly rejecting violence, the BNP was making a concerted pitch for hearts and minds. In the general election of May 1997 the BNP stood fifty candidates and was thereby able to produce a party political broadcast and distribute 2,250,000 leaflets. So in a sense the fascists in the BNP have made a clear effort to re-invent themselves as a 'respectable' 'radical' alternative within the political mainstream. Perhaps more significantly, in attempting to secure this position, they may yet be provided with political space through an emphasis on certain key issues. For example, by exploiting their conception of nationhood the BNP could quite possibly attract support in opposition to European integration, devolution, immigration levels and so on.

All of this poses difficult strategic and tactical questions for anti-fascists, particularly AFA. AFA was designed specifically to combat the physical presence of fascism, and AFA was able to differentiate itself from other anti-fascist groups by the extent to which it was successful in achieving this. Now 'the enemy' is changing and becoming far more sophisticated. As AFA's internal documentation acknowledges '... there is a serious danger that AFA, without the physical challenge for which it was designed, will itself lose direction and begin to atrophy'. [8] The problem is not so much in dealing with the threat of fascists on the streets but in constructing a tactical paradigm capable of forestalling the insidious drift of politics toward the fascists waiting on the extreme right.

In attempting to come to terms with this AFA has adopted a strategy of 'graduated and flexible response' (to borrow from the terminology of nuclear deterrence). That is, AFA has committed itself to responding to BNP initiatives at every level, even if this entails entering what might be termed 'conventional politics'. However, it must be said that in doing this AFA, given its support base and ideological disposition, remains focused on the working class. Indeed this agenda was evident in the founding documentation of AFA, which stated unequivocally that 'we are not fighting Fascism to maintain the status quo but to defend the interests of the working class'. [9] As one prominent AFA organiser put it '...our basic philosophy is that we're working-class and that ultimately we want to see working-class people organised in their own communities, making things happen for themselves' ('Anti-Fascist Action', interview 'S'). Given this explicit political orientation towards the working class, the broad 'popular front' strategy of class unity has always been viewed as unacceptable within AFA, despite its attractive simplicity. 'Popular front' approaches are considered inadequate and inappropriate because they tend to identify anti-fascism with the status quo, thereby reinforcing the impression of fascism as the radical alternative. And this particular point is critical since,

> ...the ambition of militant anti-Fascism is not just to see the threat posed by the far right to the existing political order removed, so that the social conditions that gave rise to the threat can once again be safely ignored. On the contrary, it is not for militant anti-Fascism to argue that radical change is not needed; instead our primary role is to ensure that if a successful challenge to the Establishment is mounted, it comes only from the left. [10]

In adopting this approach AFA activists have been pro-active in the setting up

---

8. AFA, 'Filling the Vacuum', Strategy Document London AFA, 27 May 1995.
9. AFA (London) Constitution Part 1.4.
10. AFA Document presented to International Conference October 1997.

of the Independent Working Class Association, which is designed to give left-wing activism a new focus and direction. Constructed upon communitarian principles, it aims to facilitate the emerging political aspirations of the hitherto marginalised working class. In attempting this, the IWCA is seeking to differentiate itself from other so-called 'revolutionary' left-wing groups by rejecting sterile 'ideological' debate and attracting the indigenous population of run-down council estates in various community- based projects. The idea is to empower local working-class communities rather than impose a pre-set agenda derived from the 'sacred texts' of Marxist theory. In this sense there is an explicit inversion of Leninist organisational principles which stress democratic centralism and the role of the vanguard party. Whether or not such a strategy is sustainable is of course open to question, but IWCA organisers can, with some justification, point to the abject failure of alternative 'left-wing' approaches.

In conclusion our evidence would suggest that AFA is more ideologically complex, tactically sophisticated and mission-committed than conventional descriptive accounts have acknowledged. Individual members are unquestionably animated by non-egoistic motives and the organisation itself provides an important reference point in terms of facilitating common purpose and the formation of political identity. In short, the simplistic 'rent-a-mob' epithet is well wide of the mark. In fact, when it comes to evaluating the role of anti-fascists in opposing the political message espoused by certain fascist groups, it would be unwise to underestimate the impact and importance of Anti-Fascist Action. However, there is no doubt that the tactical re-orientation of the BNP now presents, at least potentially, far greater challenges for AFA and indeed all those who would seek to oppose fascism.

Special needs - bullying - racism

The last taboo?

Ann Briggs

Ann Briggs reflects on the disturbing implications of her daughter's school experiences.

at the school gates ...

The wait for my daughter to come out of the school gate is a strange and unnerving experience. As it is a segregated 'special needs' secondary school (for pupils with moderate learning disabilities), most of the other children are bussed home on the special mini-buses and so there are no other parents outside the gates to greet, chat with and share experiences. Standing in isolation, with no distractions, I pass the minutes feeling the dry throat and stirring stomach that indicate the anxiety which comes on towards the end of every school day. I can tell, the minute she walks around the corner of the building, what sort of day it has been - is she running towards me, her head held high and smiling a welcome, or is she almost shuffling along, staring at the ground and reluctant to engage with me. I dread the latter; it will be a painful couple of hours or more before she finally divulges the events of the day. I know all the advice in these situations and I try to stay calm and supportive, but sometimes the bile and anger rise up inside of me and, though I know only too well that none of it belongs with her, I inevitably end up spitting it out in her direction.

in the playground ...

Was it W.E. DuBois who said 'racism doesn't happen all of the time, in every situation but it can happen at any time and in any situation'?

As a white adult parent, I have to use my imagination to reconstruct the events and feelings which Marianna does her best to describe. Of course I miss some of the nuances of the power battles and I cannot avoid putting an adult gloss on the language and images. But here goes ...

My picture of my daughter in the playground is of a generally lively, happy, sociable child - that is what she is like at home and in other social milieus most of the time - who, initially, cannot believe what is happening to her. At first, she pretends she is hearing things, or that it isn't really directed at her personally; but she is the only Black child in her class and eventually she cannot escape the message. Somehow, she knows that words such as 'baboon', 'bogeyman', 'Paki' are designed to assault her very sense of being - 'Is that me? Is that a baboon?' she asks me, pointing at the double decker sized poster of a gorilla adorning the sides of buses to advertise a *King Kong* movie. The hurt and the pain build up and build up - either to be taken out on someone even less powerful than herself, or to be bottled up inside with devastating results.

Marianna started to dread playtimes. She didn't know whether it would just be the usual daily name-calling which she was learning somehow to live with or whether it would be a really bad day and she'd have to somehow respond to the question from an older white girl whilst eating a mini chocolate Swiss roll, which I had put in her sandwich box, 'why are you eating a black man's dick?' - or games where a group of older boys run past her, throwing a punch to her stomach or, alternatively, 'touching her fanny'. 'Mummy, what does 'fanny' mean?' she asks on coming home. And then there is Paul, who traps her as often as he can on coming out of the girls' toilets and shoves his hand either down her knickers or up her jersey. And there is Carol, whose behaviour generally is somewhat uncontrolled, leading to frequent physical incidents with a number of other children. It becomes clear, over time, though, that her attacks on Marianna are both more frequent and more intense. I begin to take photographs of the bruises on her legs and neck, as well as one of the injury to her back of the hand caused by an assault with a nail. I find it weird that the act of taking the photograph helps me believe I am doing something constructive and absorbs a little of the anger.

But 'you're a black bastard because you don't have a real mummy and daddy' and 'you live in a children's home' were, for Marianna, the most gut-wrenching insults. They deeply touched an already confused and upset child, penetrating her most fundamental insecurities and attacking the very core of her sense of self.

Now, Marianna's liveliness and energy has drained away; she finds a corner of the playground where she can try and make herself invisible, standing as still as possible with her back against the wall, instinctively perhaps hoping for at least an element of protection from behind. Eyes wide open like a rabbit trapped in headlights, she hopes it will all just go away, becoming emotionally and physically rigid with the effort of simply surviving playtimes. Her best friend, of many years standing, avoids contact and sometimes gets angry with her for being a victim of something he too is powerless to challenge. The staff in the playground don't appear to notice anything amiss and she learns fast that no-one is going to come to her rescue. She becomes too frightened to 'report' what is happening to the teachers. This, in turn, is held against her and used to deny the seriousness of the impact of the experience.

There are days when the unhappiness weighs down so heavily that even Marianna's favourite out-of-school activity, swimming, is adversely affected and her body is too heavy with fear and sadness to move with her usual speed and grace through the water. Her swimming coach comments on the deterioration but tears well up in my eyes and my throat tightens because I detect a note of sympathy in her voice.

the role of the deputy head ...

The role of the deputy-head in dealing with the situation has been particularly critical, as the headteacher seemed to transfer the responsibility to him (having acknowledged to me that he did not read my letters of complaint). On one occasion, the deputy head chose to call the whole school together, making the few black boys in the school, who all happen to be in the older age range, stand up in front of the others in order 'to point out the potential folly of abusing some of the non-white (sic) big lads'. I quote directly from a letter he wrote to me, presumably on the basis that he was pleased with his actions. Not only does this action feed straight into the pervasive myths of black masculinity (which clearly abound within the school) but it potentially encourages further violence. I asked the deputy head who, in his opinion, would run the most risk of being excluded as a result of any such violence, should the black boys actually take on some kind of vigilante role. I mentioned the statistics relating to the exclusion from school of black children to support my argument - he clearly had no idea what I was talking about. And in all this, not one of the white perpetrators was, or has been since, publicly identified.

The deputy head also teaches the IT class.

'Mr Burrows made us draw a baboon on the computer screen today, Mummy'. Marianna began the story on the bus home after swimming, and to begin with I had some difficulty believing what I was hearing: 'Are you sure he didn't ask you all just to draw different animals on the computer?' The telling of the incident was now beginning to affect Marianna, and her speech became uncertain, halting in its delivery and more broken as the tears take hold. 'We all had to ... do ... it.' I ask, 'What did you do? Did you draw a baboon?' 'No', she says. 'I felt sick and I didn't do anything.'

Leaving aside the technical implications of requesting 12 year old children with learning difficulties to undertake this task, it is possible to imagine that the deputy head was trying to help by showing the class what a baboon looks like ... except he then left the room, leaving Marianna completely at the mercy of her class mates.

'What happened when he went out?' 'Everyone got up and came and stood round me ...They were all pointing and laughing at me ... They were all saying baboon, baboon ...' By now, we are both crying, still sat on the bus. I feel so impotent, so powerless to help. I want to scream at Mr Burrows, I want to do something similar to him - no, I want to do something worse. Marianna is now getting worried about me ... 'Mummy, please don't be cross ... don't cry'. Marianna did not attend school for some days after this.

so there was a meeting to discuss the bullying and racism ...

The meeting consisted of myself, the headteacher and the Local Education Authority's Head of Special Needs. The minutes of the meeting state 'On the incident with Paul, the headteacher said that this was a case of a boy chancing his arm and he and the boy's parents had been spoken to'. The headteacher acknowledged that Carol's behaviour could be problematic, but said it had improved about 100 per cent since junior school. He was not prepared to consider the implications for Marianna of a situation in which, once she had become the generally identified victim, it was as if other children felt they had permission to target her relentlessly with a whole range of different types of bullying. Any attempt on my part to discuss the racial abuse and violence was avoided altogether and there was no acknowledgement of the possible effects resulting from this level of stress and unhappiness.

The headteacher also introduced his opinion that Marianna is '"borderline" severe learning difficulties', which justified the argument that somehow her social immaturity (a phrase used several times during the meeting) was at the root of the problem. Her misdemeanours, such as belching in the face of one of the boys, became further justifications for the bullying.

The outcome of the meeting, requested specifically by myself to discuss the racism and the bullying perpetrated on her, was that the head decided to 'contact the school's educational psychologist … and ask her to observe Marianna in school to give an accurate picture of *her* social actions and also to do some testing so that an up to date picture of *her* cognitive functioning and reading ability could be obtained. This would be done as a matter of urgency …' (my italics) Thus, the victim becomes neatly identified as the focus and the spotlight remains directed on her.

during the annual school review meeting …

Four of us in the room. Everyone seems nervous. The headteacher covers up with his usual fragile bonhomie; his ubiquitous use of the adjective 'smashing' does nothing to counteract my growing prejudice that the school exists in a time warp. 'Now then,' he says, leaning forwards and addressing Marianna, 'this meeting is for you. Tell us what you like about school.' Marianna sits up straight, and enthusiastically mentions most, if not all of her lessons. I am totally impressed at her ability to be positive! The headteacher notes each of them down.

'Tell us what you don't like.'

Marianna begins confidently 'I don't like …' but then her voice trails off and she looks uncertainly at me. I smile encouragingly: 'I don't like being picked on or bullied', she continues, with commendable clarity and precision. There is silence in the room. Nothing is being written down. But Marianna's confidence is increasing and she continues: 'And I don't like my teacher drinking tea and coffee in the class room all day. And I don't like colouring in all day. I want to learn things and get proper homework like my friend next door Jack does.'

In reply, the teacher offers a huffy apology for the tea/coffee consumption and the colouring in is justified on the grounds of 'fine motor skill development'.

Marianna says she is bored with colouring in and I wonder aloud whether more handwriting, which she does with increasing proficiency at home, might not be a more stimulating alternative. I don't push the point as I am consciously trying to keep the atmosphere co-operative for Marianna's sake. However, I cannot contain myself when asked my views on her progress during the year, and my anger and frustration effectively dominate the rest of the meeting. I feel utterly trapped in a wall of so-called expertise which is constantly used to combat any of the points I raise.

some reflections so far ...

The school is a secondary special school for children with moderate learning difficulties. It seems to me that this school in particular - and maybe 'special needs education' in general - functions on the basis of two very powerful and largely unchallenged myths, both of which are potentially highly detrimental to both the well-being and the education of the children who are placed there by Education Authorities. The first is that, basically, these children don't really need any educational input because, to quote a comment made directly to me by Marianna's teacher, 'most of them will end up working for McDonalds anyway'. On an unannounced visit to the classroom, I was appalled at the state of Marianna's work drawer - a jumble of screwed up pieces of paper which were not organised into subjects and a library book which was several years beyond her reading capability. A number of the worksheets I noticed were sponsored by McDonalds, including one entitled 'How Eating Has Changed Over The Years' where the two-word answer, filled in neatly by Marianna was 'McDonalds' and 'Pizza Hut'. I received no reply to my question as to whether such sponsoring is common in all schools, or indeed in special needs schools.

Secondly, there seems to be an approach, that whatever behaviour goes on between the children is just to be expected because they all have special needs and so there is nothing much to be done about whatever goes down in the playground. Or, because they are children with learning disabilities, it simply does not matter what they do to each other. I think the staff at this school do not actually notice behaviour which elsewhere would at least be of concern and merit some attention.

More recently, a number of the officers of the LEA have expressed concern and have taken some action - for example, there is to be an inquiry into the sexual abuse in the next academic year. It is interesting, though, that the racism is not to be taken so seriously and the general tendency is always to treat the incidents I report (and have consistently reported) as if they are one-off, rather than attempting to see whether they are, as I believe, symptomatic of an overall approach to the educational needs of these children. It is difficult for me not to conclude that there is actually discrimination at work here and my daughter, together with her school mates, is receiving a vastly inferior education because of her disability. She is then further subject to the racialised and sexualised bullying. Little wonder that, last summer, she announced that she would not return in the autumn term. In spite of a direct suggestion from me that it might be beneficial, at the time of writing no-one from the authority had made any effort to talk to my daughter or to see whether there is a way they could ascertain her views as well as mine. I can only assume that to be directly aware of her feelings would only be uncomfortable for the professionals. But given the ethos of the Children Act and the subsequent emphasis on establishing the views and wishes of children and young people, this is surely neglectful.

the spelling test …

I couldn't work out what was wrong … Marianna had already told me there had been no bullying that day; indeed, she termed it 'a 10 out of 10 day'. Eventually, she told me about the spelling test .'I didn't want to tell you, Mummy, in case you got cross. But I had a spelling test today and I only got 2 words right.'

'Can you remember the words you got right?'

'Mars and Moon.'

'So what were the others. If you tell me what they are, maybe I can help you learn them.'

The words concerned included 'oxygen', 'satellite', 'telescope', 'Saturn', 'Uranus', and various others with an obvious connection to outer space. I confirmed with Jack, our 12 year old neighbour who attends a mainstream school, that spelling these words presented him with a significant degree of difficulty and 'satellite' sent several adults in search of the nearest dictionary. Especially in view of his assessment that Marianna has severe (rather than moderate) learning disabilities, I wrote to the headteacher requesting an explanation as to why she had been given words clearly beyond her abilities. I asked a rhetorical question which, looking back, indicates the depth of my frustration and despair: 'Is the idea of making her do something she is not yet capable of designed to humiliate her or to prove to me how severe her learning difficulties are? If she was genuinely expected to be able to spell these words, why could she not be helped to learn them by sending her home with a list of spellings on which she is to be tested as part of her homework, so that I could help her learn them?'. Not surprisingly, I added this letter to the pile to which I have never received a reply.

some more reflections ...

It is hard not to come to the conclusion that, certainly in this school, the underpinning educational theory consists mainly of whatever an individual teacher decides to do (or not do) on any particular day. It really is hard, from my view point, to see where any expertise is actually being deployed in the classroom, and I am left wondering whether there is not a reliance on the difficulty that most of my daughter's class mates would have, due to their communication difficulties, in describing to their parents the content of their day at school.

The generally held low expectations of children with learning disabilities is certainly exhibited by those perceived and presented as the experts who are actually charged to educate but who in practice do no more than contain and occupy the children. Perhaps most dangerously, I would argue that these attitudes are therefore almost bound to be absorbed and taken on by the parents and children themselves.

the Department of Education ...

The current stance of David Blunkett's office is that as there is an inquiry scheduled, then the LEA are doing all that they can be expected to do. There is no understanding of the complexities of the issues, nor that the lack of acceptance of some responsibility for what has happened to Marianna leaves both of us very alienated by the 'special needs' schooling system.

In order to reassure me that the government is taking bullying and racism seriously I was sent a copy of the DfEE publication entitled 'Social Inclusion - Pupil Support', which introduces itself as bringing together guidance on all aspects of schools' pastoral and disciplinary policies. In fact, the focus is almost exclusively on children excluded because of *their own* behavioural difficulties, and neither racism nor any other form of discrimination is mentioned as a potential factor in determining the extent of the inclusion or exclusion of a child. Marianna's experience shows precisely the extent to which a child can feel - and, indeed, *be* - totally excluded by such powerful, yet largely unacknowledged, factors.

On the contrary, the list of 'Groups at particular risk' (of what is not specified but presumably refers to risk of exclusion) offered by the report include, predictably enough, children with special needs, children in care, minority ethnic children and so on. There is no explanation at all as to why these particular children are at greater risk, so it is perfectly possible to deploy the interpretation that it must be due to features intrinsic to members of these groups. Thus any factors impinging from the outside - such as racism in the case of minority ethnic groups - can be safely ignored and, essentially, it is business as usual, with the victims ultimately held responsible for both their own actions and those perpetrated against them. Furthermore, the chapter on 'Children with Special Needs' defines this as solely those with difficult behaviour and stresses the need for effective early intervention. The exclusion of children with learning disabilities is not even alluded to.

some tentative conclusions ...

I would argue that each of the sites (the playground, the classroom, the meeting places, the local authority, government departments and, at times, home itself) concerned in some way with the provision of education for my daughter actually contributes to the multiple forms of exclusion which she suffers. The lack of recognition, the refusal to perceive events and incidents as anything other than isolated examples of bad practice, the insistence that the responsibility is due to her 'social immaturity', the apparent inability to communicate directly with her, are factors in ensuring her very real exclusion from her social world which are just as powerful as the actual bullying and racism enacted by the children.

My daughter has, in the past year, been abused and discriminated against on the basis of her disability, the colour of her skin, her perceived racial difference, her gender, and her adoptive status as the child of a single mother (I have no overt evidence that I am listened to less carefully as a woman, but I intuitively feel that a Mr Briggs would be treated with a greater degree of respect). Each of those with some degree of responsibility or authority in relation to 'special needs' education has consistently failed to exercise that responsibility - from the school itself to the government department with ultimate accountability. There is a complicated web of power relationships operating here, including that of parent-child, and I am left feeling that at no node within this web is there a professional prepared to attempt a serious analysis of the situation and challenge the prevailing inferiority of provision for those 'Groups at particular risk'.

Five Poems

Birds

There were rumours. That shrill at first light, thin
through the wall. Flits of shadow frantic on a curtain.

So I hung out my nut salami for the peckish, spread
crumbs about on my frosty lawn. Guaranteed result, they said.

Was it heck. A lifetime I was at that window
of myself, every mullion thumbed grey with waiting.

When finally, it happened, I was in the bath.
My mobile rang, and I got the part. Just like that.

I must have been a sight framed in my upstairs
window, stood on the pan, steaming like a man on fire

against February air gasping *Yes!* because, and,
that's when I saw them, out of nowhere, gliding in to land

- so laddish, so unreal, and me caught at the vital moment
with my cameras down - all at once: monsters intent

on the target, lumbering against air, petite swarms
of plump-breasted ones, exotics that didn't seem at home -

and I remember thinking they're meant to be extinct
this lot, but there they were all after my pathetic

slice of bread. I suppose there must have been females
among them, though I'm damned if I could tell

and apart from some half-dead author dating watercolours
I doubt if anyone alive now could say, or care.

Mario Petrucci

Rondel

Rickshaws clatter over the broken tarmac,
scatter children, skirt a hawker's display.
Mother-in-law squats slicing onions. Her toes splay
round the stand of her knife in the soot-black
kitchen where cooker and concrete walls fling back
the day's heat. A faint breeze from the doorway.
Rickshaws clatter over the broken tarmac,
scatter children, skirt a hawker's display.
A giant coughs over the city. A flick
of white cloth covers her head as the bray
of the mosque's loudspeaker ends the day:
Allahu akbar. *At home, church scarves were black.*
Rickshaws clatter over the broken tarmac,
scatter children, skirt a hawker's display.

Susanne Ehrhardt

Santa Fe, Winter

In the draught from the door
the scarlet rug flapped sharply,

a flame detached itself,
poising like a dancer,

the grand jeté
for some minutes over the San Pedros.

Day cried through my mouth,
a woman over an unlit log.

The door opened,
the rug pirouetted and glimmered.

Judith Kazantzis

Black Market

We left Australia still in our shells,
Concealed under the clothes of thieves

in improvised brassieres and knickers.
Travelling thousands of miles, to be sold

for thousands of pounds, we dodged
the customs of countries along the route.

Somehow we were not broken or spilt;
our potential to be Black Cockatoos

of the white, red or yellow tailed type
was safeguarded at the point of a knife.

Born in the front room of some crook in Powys,
we woke to life on a corduroy settee.

Above the mantelpiece a picture, showing
forests 'down under' oozing green life,

and now, when we dream backwards in our cages,
our crests stand up in black surprise.

Fabian Peake

Rings

Before my mother left, she lost both rings,
first between the sheets, then in the cracks
beneath the borrowed hospice crib. These rings
my father found by feel and safely kept

until the funeral. That day he gave
each daughter's daughter one, the elder, gold
the younger, silver with a diamond ray,
and told the story of the purchase, and showed

his band so that we saw the thicker golden
braided mate and saw my father's knuckle
thickened with arthritis. We four crowded
close. Gleaming clippers snapped the metal.

Then we saw my father shake his head
and stare at his bare hand. 'She's gone,' he said.

Joan Michelson

Singing politics, owning names

Shereen Benjamin
and Cynthia Cockburn

*The political song movement is alive and well
in Britain ...*

There is a thriving tradition of political song in Britain. Apart from the many
individual political singer/songwriters like Sandra Kerr or Leon Rosselson, there
are more than a dozen local choirs singing at political events, at benefits, on
demonstrations and pickets, or busking on the streets. They write their own
songs, and sing each other's, and are always responding to a changing political
scene with fresh words and tunes. There has been a marked growth among
them lately of small women's *a capella* groups singing a feminist repertoire.

Political choirs meet at the national street music festival which passes from
city to city, year by year. And *Raise Your Banners*, the annual festival of political
song, is another moment to hear many of these choirs - as well as a programme
of popular performers from this and other countries - and to attend workshops.

The two of us belong to Raised Voices, one of several London-based choirs.[1]
We wrote the song 'What's in a Name?' to respond to our dilemma in a
particular political moment. Raised Voices have many songs of liberation and
solidarity in our repertoire, from the Sandinista Anthem to A Gi Ya
Mozambique. But it's not every moment that they sound the right note.

National movements themselves emphasise different themes and acquire different significance at different times.

For instance, all those songs celebrating the green island of Ireland - the blood in her cornfields, the death of her martyrs - jar a little just now with the direction of moves in Northern Ireland. This is not to deny past oppression or present inequality. It's rather to listen to those many women and men living in Northern Ireland, nationalists among them, who are trying to find a new language in which to reach 'the Other' and explore the possibility of peace.

So this is a different kind of solidarity and liberation song. We sing it in solidarity with people who are trying to liberate themselves from the grip of those power elites that are reifying national identities, manipulating history, digging trenches between us and profiting from war.

One word in the song needs explanation - our use of the term 'Goy' in the last verse. Meaning 'non-Jew', it is the only one of the six 'names' in the song that's never proudly claimed by a group, but is only used by its Other. Used in the main pejoratively, signifying contempt for the Goyim, it is loaded with the pain of centuries of Jewish persecution. For that reason some Jews have said they feel uncomfortable singing the verse.

But the name Jew is also at times uncomfortable for non-Jews to speak, because in Goy-speech it likewise has often been heavy with negative meaning. Authorially, as a Jew and a non-Jew, we want this phrase the way we have written it. The line could have read 'Arab and Jew'. But that would have suggested that the problem lies with all those inimical groups out there. It's us too. And the song, after all, pins hope to the possibility of giving old names new meanings.

---

1. *Raised Voices* is a London-based political choir of women and men. We run as a co-operative, with no single leader. We don't audition, and are open to singers of all abilities. New members are always welcome. Contact Mick 0171 249 5139 or Marion 0171 561 1990, or see our website at <http://www.raised-voices.org.uk>

What's in a name

I think that the time could be near
When what's in a name
Doesn't mean quite the same
When the need to belong
Is no longer so strong
When the rage at the past
Has diminished at last.
But you can't see it from here.

I think that the time could be near
When the lies that we hear
And the scale of our fear
With the anger it feeds
And our murderous needs
Will have shifted their shape
So we find an escape.
But you can't see it from here.

When primordial claims
To exclusive domains
On the maps that we draw
Don't convince any more.
The gods are displaced
And the borders effaced ...

I think that the time could be near

When these names they abuse
We can take or refuse
Being Turk, being Kurd
Being Croat or Serb
Being Goy, being Jew
Has become something new
But you can't see it from here.

See of whom we're the tools.
See who names
See who rules
I can almost see it from here
Almost from here.

Words: Cynthia Cockburn
Music: Shereen Benjamin
RAISED VOICES July 1999

What's in a Name

Words: Cynthia Cockburn, Music: Shereen Benjamin
Raised Voices, July 1999

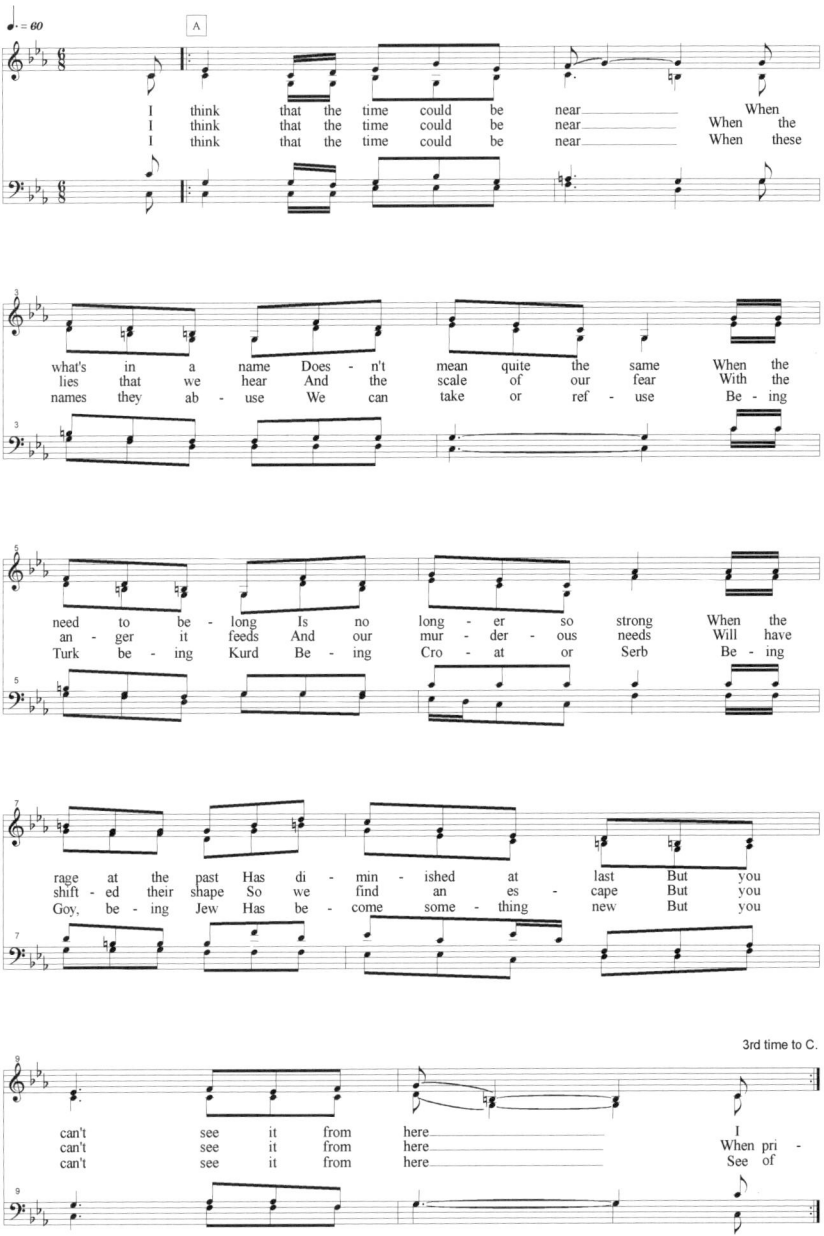

I think that the time could be near___ When
I think that the time could be near___ When the
I think that the time could be near___ When these

what's in a name Does - n't mean quite the same When the
lies that we hear And the scale of our fear With the
names they ab - use We can take or ref - use Be - ing

need to be - long Is no long - er so strong When the
an - ger it feeds And our mur - der - ous needs Will have
Turk be - ing Kurd Be - ing Cro - at or Serb Be - ing

rage at the past Has di - min - ished at last But you
shift - ed their shape So we find an es - cape But you
Goy, be - ing Jew Has be - come some - thing new But you

3rd time to C.

can't see it from here___ I
can't see it from here___ When pri -
can't see it from here___ See of

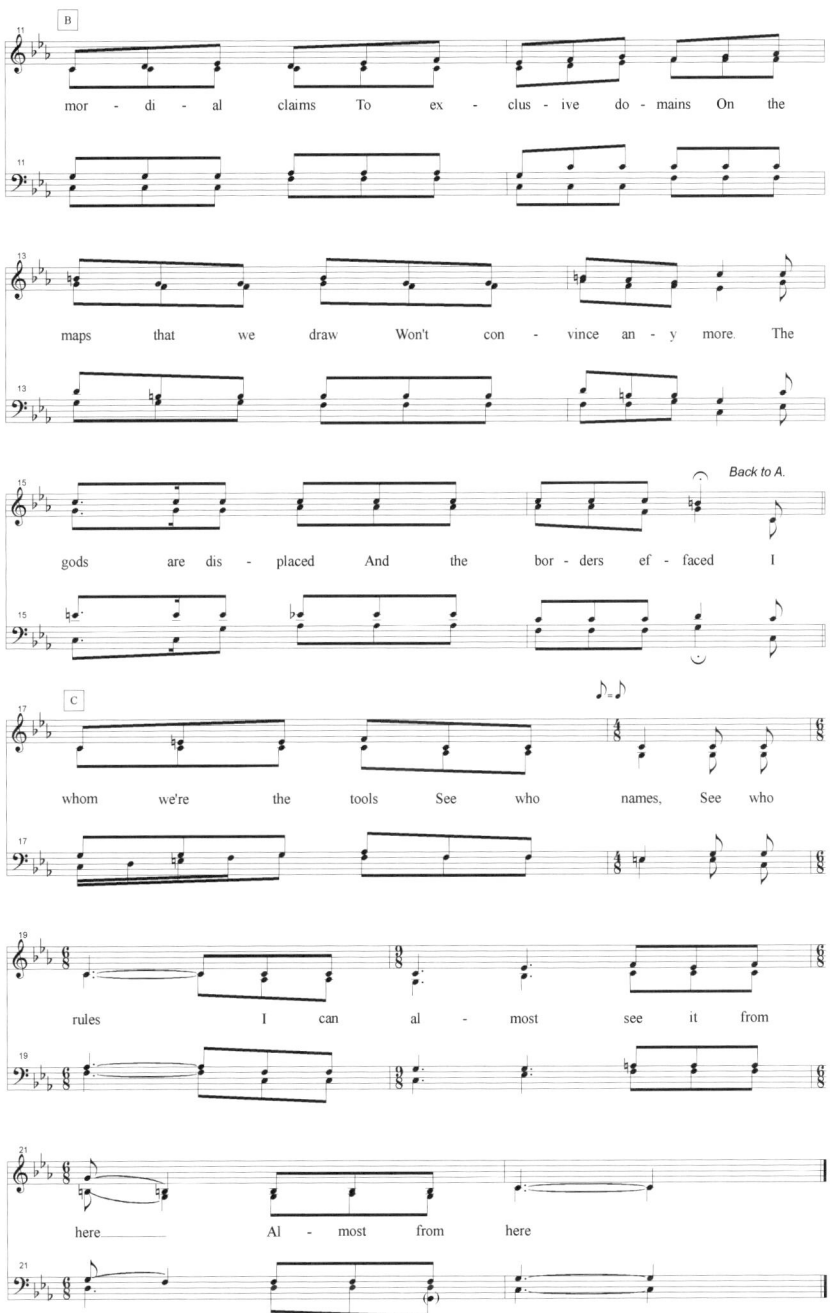

Passing shadows

Joanna Rosenthall

Short story

I drive to King's Cross. My chest burns with irritation. I stare ahead with static eyes. The traffic and the road should be taking up all my concentration. Out of the corner of my eye I am transfixed by my mother's shape. She is hunched at my side, my passenger. Her shoulders are strained upwards as if she is cold. I realise with a moment of compassion that she will never let them down again. Her shoulders are condemned to find an unnatural place somewhere near her ears, separated from her body. Her face is flattened by passing shadows followed by the full glare of the sun. She claws the air in front of her blindly in an attempt to lower the sunshade. She is holding her head stiffly to one side like a defeated bird. She is small and shrunken. I can't easily remember the woman she was when I was a child. She was tall and her hair was brown. I think she wore tight skirts with a rough weave and rayon lining which went with soft matching cardigans. Her hair is white and very permed. It sits up high on her head and sweeps round in rolls which never move.

At the traffic lights I turn my head and steal a glance. Her eyes are closed and her face is so unmoving I know what it will look like when she dies. It is an old lady's face, lined and falling but with her eyes closed it looks flat and uncomplicated like the face of a baby.

'Are you going for your hair-do after you've dropped me?' She asks this in a thick loaded voice. Her eyes are still closed.

'No. I've cancelled it.' I crunch the gears which is unusual. Normally I drive through London fast and clear about where I'm heading. A working mother. 'I'm going to see Al in hospital. You know her, the one I was at school with. You've met her so many times. She's ill. I must see her before we go away, there might not be another chance. I've already told you that.' I add the last bit in revenge because her memory is fading.

I know that she is telling me I'm too modern. I shouldn't care that much about someone else because they're not family, that my hair is too long, or is it too short? It needs 'doing'. And other things. I am not as beautiful as she was, nothing like; she was such a beauty nothing else mattered.

'Oh of course. I am forgetting everything these days,' she says in a whiny tone that pleads for my sympathy. I struggle a bit, searching, but it evades me.

'Will you phone Ruth? Tell her which train I'm on. It's the 11.50. She can ring the station and find out what time it gets in.' The emphasis is on the 'she'. There's a pause and I know what's coming next. 'She didn't ring me for several weeks, you know, and it coincided with when I had flu. It's not that I mind that. When you're on your own that's one of the things you have to face, being ill. She can't help that. Of course she can't. But when weeks go by and I don't hear a thing. Why can't she pick up the phone and say look I'm busy or something? If only she'd say something it wouldn't be quite so bad.'

She waits for my reply. I offer a reluctant grunt and she launches into further complaints. It's all about her friend. She's seventy-nine and she's got a best friend. If she weren't my mother I would be able to hear the pain. She's always owed something. She did so much for Ruth years ago. Gave her money, looked after her babies, brought her wonderful things back from holidays. Exotic things that Ruth and her family would never have had. Of course that's a long time ago now and relationships don't work like that, she knows that, she tells me. But even so … it's not right. Nothing's right. Nobody looks after old people any more and I wince because there's some truth in that.

I wonder briefly for a moment what would make it better. A husband? That's what it is. I wish vehemently for a moment that my mother had a husband.

'You're too critical,' I say.

'No I'm not. You always say that. But you're wrong. I'm not. How do you think *you* would feel?'

'It's not just now. You've always judged people. I can remember you and Ruth talking over my head. I must have been eight or nine. You were always criticising. Pointing out people whose babies weren't bathed every day.'

I stop. I realise I have spoken without thinking. Something urgent within me has pushed and pushed and this has burst out. And now I am criticising her too.

My mother is entirely silent. I have judged her harshly. My stomach contracts.

It feels squeezed. Lurching. I know I've done something dreadful and I can't retract it. Maybe I want to say sorry. Not sorry for what I've said but sorry I am so angry. But I don't. I'm in pain for causing her pain.

For a moment I lose myself. I am eight. I am with my mother and her friend. I love being with them. I am safe. There are lots of home-made cakes and tea. We are in a room on the ground floor at the back of the house. Outside it is totally quiet. Inside the curtains are summer yellow and covered in flowers. The wallpaper is the identical design and I can't take my eyes off the line where the curtains become the wall. I haven't seen decor like this in anyone else's house so I know I am in a very special place. I am listening intently. As far as I am concerned these two safe women will always be there unravelling things. They talk about people. They know so much, who is related to who, what people have done and what is right and what is wrong. How do they know? I am deeply puzzled. I look for some flicker of all this inside myself. Nothing at all. How will I come to learn these things? There seems to be nothing inside me that would lead to it.

I wanted to be certain about everything too. That's how little I knew.

Suddenly she is a little old lady sitting next to me. I realise that she won't be here forever, in fact her death feels imminent. I'm pulling into the station now and I fervently wish that there was further to go. There's a big black taxi in front of me. It stops in the middle of the road blocking my way. I don't mind at all. I want to have all the time in the world sitting in the car with my mother at my side.

'I'm not judgmental,' my mother repeats. Her voice is no longer harsh, more questioning. She longs for me to forgive and forget. So do I. 'At least not much anyway,' and then after another pause, 'I'm not as bad as Ruth.' She really believes that and I want to laugh. As she speaks she jerks her chin upwards and forwards as if Ruth is over there and she is indicating her whereabouts. She doesn't want to attack me back. Perhaps at seventy-nine things have started to look a little different or perhaps she doesn't want a row just before we part.

I walk slowly down the platform with her, carrying her holdall. Neat little overnight bag. She wants to get on at the first carriage that isn't first class. I resist. I want to find her the best seat at a table and facing in the right direction. She fights back and suddenly I realise that she is tired. She doesn't want to walk any more.

I hesitate to put her bag on the overhead rack. How will she get it down? 'Please put my bag up there on the rack,' she orders. 'I'll ask someone to help,' she adds and smiles. Smirks really. I can see that she is bitter that I am worrying because for this moment I am here to worry but most of the time so much happens and I'm not there. I have moved away. She manages without me.

She walks back down the carriage with me to the door of the train. I turn to kiss her.

'I love you,' she says. Her voice is soft and nuzzly.

'I love you too,' I say quietly, my voice sounds flat as if I don't mean it. I do mean it but I need to convey that I might mean something different to her. 'That seems pretty lucky,' I add deliberately raising the tone of my voice.

'I know,' she says, 'travel is so easy these days.' I don't tell her that she has completely misunderstood me. It would involve repeating things that are too tender. We agree that I shouldn't wait for the train to leave because I need to visit Al and get home to cook. I walk away. I stop once or twice to wave but after the first time she goes and sits down.

I am walking up the platform thinking of all the things I didn't say. I am burdened by an enormous thankyou, for what I am not quite sure. I should thank her more. I feel the imminence of a time when she won't be here to thank and I am already feeling that I have been left with all the yearning.

I am thinking about a doll that sits shrouded in dust on my desk at the top of the house. I picked it up, earlier today, absent-mindedly and the feather cape disintegrated all over my hands. The white desk is covered with fine black hairs that strike me as insanitary. The grass skirt is intact but the legs are very loose. I pull one gently and it comes away in my hands. The remains of a rigid green rubber band are stuck to the top of it. The doll has Maori paintings on her face and a queer green charm tied round her neck which has heart-shaped lips and red eyes. I turn her over and see that she has moths eggs in her hair. The back of her head is bald. They have not eaten the glue which stuck the hair on. I hesitate, holding her over the bin.

We wait for him. The whole family stuck on an intake of breath, waiting. I am up late. Very late because we are waiting for him. He doesn't come. I am confused. I'm not sure if he lives with us any more. I have to go to bed. I walk up the stairs slowly because my calves are aching. The sheets are cold. I wake in the middle of the night. It is quiet but someone is very near. My father is bending over me and I sit up quickly as if it were the morning. My father's breath is right in my face, a familiar warm organic swirl of ingested whisky and cigarettes. He is sobbing. I love you so much, he says, which makes my stomach go tight. He reaches out with one of his hands and I am wondering where it will land. His hand is shaking like the awful sobs coming out of his mouth. It bumps heavily onto my shoulder and I am rigid. I am frightened of what he will do next. I lie down again and pretend that I have not been awake. He stays on my bed for a long time and I watch him in the dark through slits in my eyes.

In the morning my father has left but the doll is on my shelf wrapped in an airport bag which is stiff and crinkly. The next time I see him he tells me that the green smiling thing around her neck is a lucky charm called a Tiki.

The doll is reprieved. I lay her down on the edge of the desk and tell myself to bring a cloth up here to wipe away the mess.

At the end of the platform I turn right. It is a sunny day and I watch people as they walk towards me and then round me, almost touching. I stride up to the call box taking pleasure in not slowing down right up until the last minute. I have Al's phone number in the back pocket of my jeans. I dial. It rings two or three times. I can see her room in the hospice. The telephone is at the side of the bed on a table with wheels. Her voice is slurred.

'I'm so drowsy,' she says. It sounds as if she has dropped the phone onto her chest and her chin is crunched into her neck. I can see her in my mind at a table in a cafe where we are meeting. She is reading a book as I rush in ten minutes late. She looks up. She has kind eyes and thin hair and she is smiling at me a wide even smile, with shining tomb-stone teeth.

'Are you,' I say, 'I'm so sorry, I'm so sorry. I thought I'd come and see you.'

'I can't see you now,' she says, 'I can't.' She sounds drunk and faraway. I look around at people walking into the station. They all seem to be laughing and wearing shorts.

Relief floods me. I'm not going to the hospital to see a dying woman. She has already ceased being Al.

I run back through the station thrilled and agile, feeling like a teenager, darting away from slow-moving people with suitcases. The train is still there! I'm running all the way down Platform 8 to the carriage where my mother is sitting. I see her through the window. I am panting. Her white head is peering into a newspaper. I knock hard onto the window. Ninety seconds to departure. A lot of heads turn including hers. I indicate the door which has thick glass and is electronically closed. We stand on opposite sides of it mouthing to each other.

'Al - i - son doesn't want me to go,' I say, wildly exaggerating the lip movements.

'That's a relief,' she mouths smiling.

I nod vigorously. I wish I was different and didn't feel quite so relieved. When I stop my vision is blurred.

'I'll ring you,' she says holding her hand to her ear in a most modern way, using her thumb and little finger to imitate the shape of a telephone receiver. I can suddenly see a picture of her using a mobile phone and I want to laugh through the middle of wanting to cry. The crying starts to get the upper hand because I can't tell her any of it. Then she looks at me like a mother does to her crumpled child. There is nothing she wouldn't do for me.

I am staring at my mother's hands. I am on her knee but facing away from her, perhaps embarrassed because I am already too big to be there unquestioningly. My own knees stretch far away from me and my feet easily touch the floor and yet I feel I am dangling. My mother's hands are clasped in front of me, they are holding me on. Now and again she heaves me and herself and I am rearranged into a better position but not comfortable. She is talking to someone else, perhaps it is my aunt. Every so often she speaks to me. You are too big to be on my knee really, she says, but she doesn't slacken her grip and I don't want to get off. I finger her hands, swivelling her rings, loving the shape of the square green stone she wears. With my palms I squeeze her two hands, forcing them as close together as they will go. They are deeply interwoven. Then I gently pull each one to test whether they are firmly stuck and she resists me as if she knows my game. Time stretches ahead of me in a flat empty plain. Needing something new I gently lift the skin from the back of her hand making a small mountain ridge. Then I let it go, watching it slowly resettle.

The air smells of trains and it lies still in the tunnel of the platform. She is saying something else now. I can't understand it. Her lips are stretching and contracting in fast succession. She looks like a clown pretending to speak. Mouthing nonsense. Her mouth suddenly comes to a resting position and when I look up at her eyes her face is expectant and smiling as if she thinks I have understood. I have not. She repeats the whole thing again. I am looking hard at her mouth but no sense comes out of it. She repeats this again maybe three more times. I am baffled. My forehead is wrinkled and my cheeks pinched with incomprehension. She gives up and indicates with a curved arm movement and a pointed finger that she will tell me later.

It's practise,' she's saying. 'It needs a lot of practise,' her eyes are looking upwards to emphasise her point. Then she pats her breast smugly to tell me that she is good. She can lip-read. She is much better than me.

'You're not very good at lip-reading,' she mouths, delighted. I get that. That's easy.

A whistle blows and the train makes a different noise. In spite of this it is unexpected when it slowly glides off. I look up at her and blow her a kiss.

Sen for Americans?

Maureen Mackintosh

Amartya Sen, *Development as Freedom*, Oxford University Press £17.99

Amartya Sen is one of the world's most renowned - and most unusual - economists. In a hugely productive academic career - whose full influence on the subject of economics I hope that we have yet to see - Sen has persistently sought to bring ethical concerns into the centre of economics.[1] He has attacked with philosophical reasoning the strongly held view in economics that human action must be understood as motivated primarily by self-interest. He has held a chair at Harvard in Economics and Philosophy, and has brought philosophers and economists together.[2] As a nine year old child in Dhaka, he witnessed the Bengal famine (p180), and his policy-related work - much of it concerned with the problem of hunger - has sought to demonstrate that something can be done, even at low income levels, about 'deprivation, destitution and oppression' (pxi).

That Sen's mix of highly abstract theoretical achievement and relentless focus on the alleviation of poverty should be unusual says much about the nature of economics as a profession. That Sen should have finally been awarded, in 1998, the Nobel Prize in Economic Science is cheering. This recognition has also provided a moment for taking his ideas to a wider audience. Despite his deep involvement with development policy, Sen is very much an academic who has, as he puts it in the preface to *Development as Freedom*, 'throughout my life, avoided giving advice to the "authorities" ... preferring to place my suggestions

---

1. A lucid and accessible earlier exposition is *On Ethics and Economics* Blackwell 1987.
2. See for example *The Quality of Life*, edited by Sen and the philosopher Martha Nussbaum, Clarendon Press 1993.

and critiques - for what they are worth - in the public domain' (pxiv). *Development as Freedom* brings together a range of his work in 'a general work on development ... aimed particularly at public discussion' (pxiii). The book began life as a series of lectures given to the World Bank in 1996, an origin that appears - as discussed below - to have shaped the presentation of the ideas in some interesting ways.

The readership of *Soundings* would seem a good example of the broader audience Sen may have had in mind, and the book does offer a good way into Sen's work. But beginners starting here should be warned: the book is surprisingly uneven in tone and analytical content, infuriatingly repetitive in places, and lacks some of Sen's characteristic clarity and focus. This review aims to offer reasons why general readers might want to tussle with this book, by introducing a few of Sen's most influential arguments as re-presented here, and to reflect briefly on what is new here - the *reframing* of many of these arguments in terms of 'freedoms'.

Perhaps Sen's single most important theoretical argument with a bearing on policy has been his response to what economists call the problem of 'interpersonal comparison of utilities'. The dominant view in economics holds that the benefits or pleasures gained by different people from - say - consuming food cannot be compared. All we know is what they choose, not whether one person is made happier, or better off, than the other by the choice. This theoretical starting point trails a long tail of consequences, including a relatively low priority within economics[3] given to the analysis of inequality (since that involves comparing people). A further consequence has been the narrowing of many economists' analysis of poverty to the measurement of low real incomes, reducing policy in turn to seeking to put more cash in people's hands.

Sen has tackled that whole theoretical mind-set head on, drawing on some very old traditions in economics, from Aristotle via Adam Smith, of concern with ethics and valuation. His proposed solution to the problem of comparison has been an analysis of people's well being - specifically, of what it is to be poor - in terms not of income but of what income is *for*, that is, what people are able to do and be. As he puts it here, 'poverty must be seen as the deprivation of basic capabilities rather than merely as lowness of income'(p87). By 'capabilities'

---

3. At one point Sen disputes this, saying 'economists as a group cannot be accused of neglecting inequality as a subject' (p107) but his list of references on the topic is strikingly short compared with his lengthy lists on other topics. Leading economics *texts* notably downplay the topic.

Sen means something quite close to the concept of 'opportunities' in our common parlance notion of 'equal opportunities': in Sen's words, 'the ability ... of people to live lives they have reason to value and ... the real choices they have'(p293). 'Real' here is an important qualifier of 'choices': Sen has long argued that acute deprivation and social restriction deprive people of aspiration and energy, so by asking about preferences we gain limited information about well being. 'Capability deprivation' thus includes premature mortality, frequent illness, illiteracy, lack of access to employment, lack of civil rights, and lack of respect.

The radical implication of this perspective has been the reworking of dominant measures of poverty in more direct forms, rather than relying solely on income measures. The influential United Nations *Human Development Reports* have taken just this approach (led, as Sen is quick to note, by others such as the Pakistani economist Mahbub ul Haq). Sen has used the capability approach to argue that extreme poverty in the sense of capability deprivation is related to low incomes, but in complex ways that need to be understood. Thus, very low incomes in South Asia and sub-Saharan Africa - the poorest areas of the world - are associated with diverse patterns of deprivation in terms of mortality, illiteracy, oppression and lack of civil rights. Life expectancy, though low, is longer in India (60 years in 1991) than in Africa (52 years), and the median age at death, low in India at 30, was *five* in sub-Saharan Africa in the early 1990s. On the other hand around *half* of India's children are malnourished, twice the rate found in sub-Saharan Africa(p102). And while relative neglect (and worse) of girl children and young women in India produces, on various estimates, 20 to 40 million 'missing women' in India (displayed in low ratios of women to men in the population), such relative deprivation of women appears virtually absent in sub-Saharan Africa. Finally, a different example comes from the US: African-American women have more than twice the mortality of white women, *adjusted for incomes*, and have a life expectancy lower than women in the southern Indian state of Kerala despite vastly higher real incomes (adjusted for cost of living differences) (pp21-2, 96-7).

The further radical implication of this analysis is that something can be done. Sen has persistently argued - notably in work with Jean Dreze - that 'public action' is effective.[4] Direct provision of elementary education and primary health

---

4. *Hunger and Public Action*, edited by Dreze and Sen, Clarendon Press 1989.

care, and the removal of restrictions on women's participation in social and economic life, act directly to relieve poverty (and stimulate growth) at low income levels. Provision of emergency public employment is dramatically effective in preventing famine(p177) .

> What makes ... widespread hunger even more of a tragedy is the way we have come to accept and tolerate it as an integral part of the modern world, as if it is a tragedy that is essentially unpreventable (in the way ancient Greek tragedies were) (p204).

Furthermore - and here we move into the particularity of this book - Sen argues that other elements of public culture and human agency create pressure for benign public action, notably critical media and public debate, the effective operation of democracy and the extent of social empowerment of women. As he puts it (several times), 'famines do not occur in democracies' (p51).

This is where the 'freedom' theme of this book takes hold. Sen has extracted the themes in his earlier work concerning the importance of human agency, democracy, and open debate, and brought them into the foreground by *relabelling* his concept of capabilities as 'substantive freedoms' and then characterising these as the ends of development: 'the success of a society is to be evaluated ... mainly by the substantive freedoms that members of that society enjoy' (p18). The 'means' of development are then similarly relabelled, as 'instrumental freedoms' (pp38-9): including civil rights ('political freedoms', 'participatory freedom' (p32)); access to economic resources, including freedom of employment and exchange, and to 'social opportunities' such as health care (both included in 'the freedom to survive' (p43)); 'transparency guarantees' (such as a norm of business trust and public disclosure of information); and some level of social security from destitution ('the freedom to avoid economic disasters' (p51)). As the relabelling as 'freedoms' proceeds, it becomes awkward and over-inclusive, as the last phrase illustrates.

By this point, readers may be wondering if clarity of analysis is not getting lost behind - perhaps - a sales pitch? This book began life, remember, as lectures for the World Bank. It can be read as a sustained effort to get attention from the US-dominated culture of the Bank for the core arguments of Sen's work. Relabelling public action *and* its purposes as 'freedoms' may make them seem more worthy of American attention? The World Bank tends to operate by shifting from one 'big idea' to another, banging them home in its influential *World Development Reports*. To the extent that this reframing of Sen's work adds to pressure within the Bank for policy that abandons 'the underlying - and often unargued - belief that has been dominant in some policy circles that human development is really a kind of luxury that only richer countries can afford (p.143) - I wish the sales pitch very well.

But in fact this is not all there is to the reframing, which grows directly out of the foundations of Sen's work, both in his emphasis on *agency* - on a view of people as active shapers of their lives, not passive 'patients' - and in his individualism. This *is* an individualist view of the world, that identifies individual freedom as the objective of development, and then goes on to argue that freedoms interact in benign ways, democracy and liberty sustaining social provision and interacting in a virtuous circle with freedom of exchange. This is an argument, in essence, that individual freedoms can sustain and be sustained by social democratic institutions - although never labelled as such - even at low levels of income, and thereby also generate economic growth. The argument in favour of freedom, democracy and civil rights is addressed directly at times to those, such as the former president of Singapore, Mr Lee Kwan Yu, who have argued that authoritarianism is required for economic development, and to those who argue that 'Asian values' privilege order over liberty. There are moments when the book seems astonishingly optimistic, given the evidence it confronts, a testament to a much more honourable and socially committed tradition of liberalism than the market liberalism of the 1980s, and one with roots in many cultures of the world.

The individualism in turn creates weaknesses and absences in this book. A ghost at the feast is collective action in all its forms. Sen recognises here the importance of *how* democracy functions (p159), of the norms that shape business behaviour (pp263-5), and of non-governmental public action (p116). But political parties feature scarcely at all (there is a mention of the importance of political opposition) and trades unions not at all despite their important influence on the terms of employment. The book emphasises the importance of non-market institutions (p116) but the role of organised action by the dispossessed in contesting inequality is virtually absent. As a result the historical origins of existing social democratic provision of health and education in political struggle and trade union mutuality - and some of the sheer political nastiness of that history - is hidden.

So this *is* 'Sen for Americans', but not only that. It is a compelling view of development, which challenges those of us with comfortable lives and long life expectancies to recognise the extreme freedoms these entail. It is attractive in its foundational assumption of the equal worth of people: for instance, Sen's assumption that women's lesser freedoms are unarguably unjust (as well as arguably unproductive of development) is sufficiently unusual in the writings of male economists to be truly startling to the inured female reader. That it leads on to unanswered questions is an indicator of a good book.

Model men
Helen Crowley

Susan Faludi, *Stiffed*, Chatto and Windus

In her previous book, *Backlash*, Susan Faludi charted the entrenched resistances to the feminist project to transform the prevailing gender order. In *Stiffed* her aim was to attempt to find out from men themselves why they were so committed to resisting changes that would ultimately benefit them as much as women. What she found, however, was that she had started off on the wrong path. The stories the men had to tell her detailed a quite different landscape of power, the myriad lines of which mapped a bleak cultural reality that enveloped and emasculated men. In this new world order which Faludi explores - above all else a quintessentially American world - masculinity had become problematised in ways that went beyond the embittered patriarchal dethronement she had anticipated finding. The much-touted crisis in masculinity masked another deeper malaise, and it is the strength of the book that Faludi is able to reach this subterranean level of cultural alienation, and to recount a story that is both engaging and sobering as well as politically optimistic and open-ended.

The concept of understanding *men's* place in late modernity, however, also contains the book's weakness; the analysis is burdened with the cumbersome and unwieldy analytic preconceptions of an unreconstructed feminism, and this sometimes blunts some of its sharper insights and political instincts. Having said that, it should be acknowledged that Faludi manages to convey some of the passion and energy that fuelled the earlier ambitions of feminism; she thus provides a reminder that, crude as the truths expressed by social movements are, they have a soundness and depth which can be lost in the process of philosophical reflection and theoretical refinement.

The sheer volume of the stories she amasses is impressive; and she is attentive to the cadences of the disparate voices to which she listens. On occasion the retelling is so evocative that it elicits a real sense of recognition of a moment, or of a structure of feeling.

Faludi interviews men whose lives have been reshaped in the process of de-industrialisation, or defined by the horrors of the war in Vietnam. She talks to those who, discarded by the new managerialism, attempt to negotiate the constantly changing rapids of the de-industrialised labour market, or try to engage with the image machinery of a media-saturated society. In so doing, she has assembled a set of narratives that chart the shift from the centred, hegemonic, cultural universe of America in the 1950s and 1960s to the ambivalences and volatilities of late modernity. This is achieved with great effect, and Faludi conveys a real sense of the personal costs exacted by such restructurings.

However, there is no discussion about how the narratives were selected or why. In one sense to raise these issues is nit-picking since it is not an academic book: it is more a political intervention. Nevertheless, her selection does have a discernible logic, and the failure to make this explicit causes problems. The problem lies not in the narratives that Faludi includes, but in the stories that are excluded - those of the victors of the transition to a post-colonial world. The real power brokers, the Wall Street suits, the information economy commanders, the one-man multinationals, the defence industry barons, the fiscal arbitrators … these are not represented in this story about 'men': hers is a story only about certain kinds of men. Since Faludi does not acknowledge any selection criteria, the implicit argument is that she has drawn 'modern man' sufficiently broadly to allow for generalist conclusions.

This undifferentiated concept of 'modern man' also contains another of the book's unmarked projects - the attempt to find a resolution of the gender wars through the advocacy of an alliance between women and men; this alliance would battle for 'humanness', against the dehumanising power of the market. In some sense this composite project succeeds - certainly it cannot simply be dismissed on the grounds of its unreconstructed feminism, or inattention to historical resonance. But her project is flawed because not only does she bury class in her appeal to 'modern man', she also foregoes any analysis of what used to be called capitalism. Ultimately, the concept of 'modern man' is an unsuitable Trojan horse to carry the book's covert ambitions. Her exclusion of modern man the victor is a crucial weakness, since it is the victors, not the market, who are the others of the vanquished.

The men to whom Faludi talks are men who have been economically marginalised by de-industrialisation: they are men rendered psychically and emotionally illiterate by their fundamentalist commitment to a cultural order that has been disassembled, almost literally, before their eyes. They are erstwhile working men, who understood themselves to have produced and defended the material and cultural world they occupied, and were rewarded - and found identity - within the terms of its inclusiveness. (Within this group some bear witness to just how remorseless and exacting the terms of inclusion were, but Faludi is more preoccupied with inclusiveness than with the markers of exclusion.)

Faludi also detects in these reminiscences a more disabling sense of impoverishment, generated by the recognition that a bogus ethics of manhood had promised values and status but delivered only abandonment in a world of emotional illiteracy and post-colonial brutality. And she has a deep sympathy with this sense of abandonment. But underpinning her account is a view that men's place in an order of systemic oppression can be best understood empathetically. This is hardly a new argument and makes up the substance of many alliances across gender boundaries. However, this approach ignores a lesson that has been hard won by many feminists: that a sense of being 'done to' does not constitute the terms of political abrogation; rather, it marks the passage to recognition of the other, and a sense of self that is relational and not individualistic. Acknowledgement of one's placing in regimes of power represents for many feminists a crucial way to understand the politics of cultural identity. But this is an insight which Faludi seems unconcerned to deploy, and her analysis is the weaker for it.

The other inflection of modern man that Faludi traces is that voiced by those actual and aspiring 'culture workers' who are more directly caught up in the world of ornamental masculinity, in which image and media exposure are the currency of the new symbolic economy. Like women before them, men are objectified by the ornamental culture - including those involved in the sex industry. The depths to which masculinity can be pushed in these areas leads Faludi to pose her final question: why is it that men are unable to mobilise themselves in their own defence in the way that women did. The early women's movement resisted encroaching consumerism and objectification, and tried to think through exactly what femininity and masculinity meant. They named men as the colluders and upholders of patriarchy - at least in Faludi's very American rendition. Men, she suggests, provided feminism with an object and a strategy - men were the enemy and it was the task of women to wrest power from them. Many men, however, as Faludi's subjects testify, were in the process of losing what little power they had at the hands of the same forces that enabled women to make claims for a greater equality. Feminists, like civil rights activists before them, were to discover the limits of a strategy of blaming and began the task of acknowledging how complex are the workings of power. Faludi argues that men don't resist in the same way as women did because they don't have an enemy to blame. But although this arrests the process of resistance, it also abets it, in the sense that the absence of an enemy can allow men to make alliances with others who translate loss into political ambition for a greater humanity. She argues that the project for men is not to resolve the 'crisis in masculinity' but to reclaim their masculinity in 'figuring out how to be human'.

Having started with men she ends with them, and certainly there is no quarrel to be had with her conclusions. However, along the way some of the men, the men of the market, the men not in crisis but in the fulsome identification with the formidable power of capital, have been left forgotten. She is right to suggest that the civil rights movement, the women's movement and the gay and lesbian movements have taught us to respect the human dimensions of politics and the psychic obstacle course through which change must be plotted. And it is surely the case that the crisis of masculinity has produced a deeper understanding amongst women as well as men of how complex are the reverberations of othering, and how distorted the possibilities of identification across difference. But she fails to consider whether the enormously productive system of capitalism which worked so successfully through the old identities of masculinity and femininity cannot continue to do so through different and more diversified terms of belonging, still rendering women and men as its subjects. Many women, and some men, have become disaffected, and their ongoing and more inclusive regroupments remain a source of hope. But it is as well to remember that capital anoints the powerful as well as abandoning the redundant; it is the humanness of power that needs to be understood, not just the humanity of those who have no power.

A critical enchantment
Stephen Frosh

Wendy Wheeler, *A New Modernity?* Lawrence and Wishart, £13.99

It is just possible that magic is returning to the world, that in Wendy Wheeler's phrase, postmodernity is finally moving into a phase of 're-enchantment'. Evoking something new in the conclusion to her book, she writes:

> At the end of a 300 year long attempt to disenchant the world, we slowly come to recognise that we are the world and the world is us, and life is a constant process of creative interchange between body and soul (p168).

Following Bauman, whose understanding of modernity and the postmodern lies in this tension between disenchantment and re-enchantment, Wheeler develops a sustained argument about the possible relationship between 'old' (Enlightenment) and 'new' modernity in terms of neglect versus incorporation of emotion and, alongside this, rational versus ecological consciousness.

Old modernity managerialises, controls, tries through a utilitarian approach to distil knowledge in such a way that its irrational elements fall away. The gain here is an 'unbinding', in which mechanical inventiveness, instrumentalism and analytic thought are freed from the constraints of tradition; the loss is of meaning, of linkage and complexity, of human feeling. By now, the impact of this loss has become so obvious, and the intellectual fragility of the Enlightenment model so transparent, that a new modernity has begun to emerge. This can take hold of the now dead Enlightenment mentality and sacralise it, making it magical through allowing back in the virtues of more holistic modes of thought and experience. What this represents, in fact, is a breakdown in the Cartesian body/ mind split and a growing recognition of the 'creative complexity of the world', including the world inside our heads.

The familiarity of this argument should not breed contempt for the book. Wheeler takes the re-enchantment theme and combines it with Freud's opposition between two responses to loss - mourning and/versus melancholia. The latter is the state of mind characteristic of old modernity, the former, refracted through the Kleinian synthesis, is potentially the mode of response to be found in postmodernity.

Loss of any treasured thing - and particularly of 'big' things like certainty, tradition and God - is profoundly traumatising. The melancholic's response is a refusal to let go, in which the lost object is 'kept' through internalisation, but also punished for going away. Melancholia is, thus, characterised by punitive and vicious self-loathing, and by an inability to let go and move on. The mourner on the other hand, although always utterly transformed by the loss of what was once held dear and depended upon, is able to transform the shattered fragments of an earlier self and world, and to build something new from those fragments and ruins (p165).

Wheeler suggests that this mourning process has been becoming more dominant in the last quarter of a century - an optimistic portrayal of integrative progress encouragingly at odds with versions of the world in which arid, manipulative and bureaucratic narcissism triumphs. 'The old cartesian divide is in the process of giving way to more complex holistic models of both the individual's understanding of the relationship between mind and body and, more widely, the relationship between individual creatures and the living world of which they are a living part' (Ibid).

Wheeler's canvas in this text is large although predominantly British: Raymond Williams, Donald Winnicott, Graham Swift (written about beautifully), Tony Blair (not quite the same), neuroscience. Swift's novel *Last*

Orders, a pilgrimage in which one friend is laid to rest by others, is the dominant emblem of the book, its central point and the source of much energy, with its compelling evocation both of fragmentation and loss, and of community and reparation. This, for Wheeler, is the flesh on Freud's 'mourning': where easy retreat into past certainties is no longer available, it is still possible to struggle towards new modes of integrity and integration, in which what is damaged and lost can be accepted and lived with or through, taken up into new patterns of living. Partly because of the power of Swift's narratives, even in the outline form which Wheeler gives them, *A New Modernity?* has something to lean on which gives it solid support. That this should be someone else's words, a set of stories retold, is perhaps appropriate in this book about complex concern, retellings and rebuilding.

There is a lot to be said in favour of the growing appreciation of the complexity of human psychological functioning, recognisable in contemporary neuroscience as well as in the 'mourningful' apparatus which Wheeler extols in Swift's work. It is clearly the case that attitudes to politics and management, to gender and to science, are appreciably more fulfilling when they are based on the idea that emotion and rationality have to be put in relationship with one another, not sliced apart. The idea that all progress depends on the suppression of emotion - visible in the childcare practices of recent historical times as well as in the grander social constructions of industry and masculinity - is one which has caused vast damage.

Perhaps equally destructively, the unbridled appeal to emotion, dispensing with rational thought, is not limited to the wacky extremes of New Ageism: it has also fed fascism. So bringing together these poles, or rather, dispensing with the idea of an intellect-emotion polarity, is an important move. In this regard, Wheeler's espousal of Winnicottian psychoanalysis is apposite and fashionable, in that it explicitly deals with the necessary emotional conditions for thinking creatively, and the importance of secure and whole relationships for the growth and deepening of the self.

What is less clear is whether recognising complexity is quite the same thing as theorising a new modernity or, for that matter, whether exhortation towards holism (or   'ecological consciousness') is the key to a deeper appreciation of the connections to be found between bodies and minds in the world. It is interesting that Wheeler uses the terminology of 'enchantment' to frame this material, suggesting something magical at a time when things spiritual seem to be very much on the agenda even for radical critics of society. This development is almost certainly a response to the failings of Enlightenment modernity of the kind Wheeler discusses, representing a wish to make non-reductive links with other people and other material objects, mostly outside the confines of organised religion.

However, there must also be a danger that the 'enchantment' idea leads to a loss of awareness of the dangers of idealising mystical contact; to my mind, there is something healthy about mistrusting modes of communication which operate outside rationality. As noted above, this is not to gainsay the claim that emotion and reason should be in closer company with one another; it is only to register caution about knowing too much too soon.

Overall, then, this is an engaging and provocative book, ranging over a variety of material, congruent with an attempt to construct a post-modern understanding in which some of the old, sad polarities are overcome. It is more part of the solution than part of the problem, because it alerts us to the possibilities for new growth in this enchanting direction. In the end, like most books of this kind, it is a moral tale; a new ethics of mourning might not on the face of it be much of a clarion call, but it does make for more complex and complete thought.

One-dimensional politics

INTRODUCTION

One-dimensional politics

Wendy Wheeler

There's something Humpty-Dumpty-ish about New Labour these days - and it's not simply the possibility of a fall and the pride which precedeth it. It's the strange way that, like Humpty, who thought he could make words mean what he wanted them to ('When I say 'glory' I mean a good knock-down argument'), New Labour thinks that it can make the word 'shambles', for instance, mean 'The Dome's millennium night was a great success'; or that 'what Robert Winston meant was that the NHS is still suffering from the Tories' funding cuts'. How is it that, for the great realists in government - who insist that the country must face, and embrace, the real hard facts of the modern world and globalisation - reality can so easily slip its anchor? Or that the relationship between experiences and the words supposed to describe them can come so strangely adrift? Is there a radical social constructionist somewhere deep in the bowels of Number Ten, telling the politicians that the entire world is simply linguistically constructed, and that to say a thing is so is to *make* it so? If George Orwell were alive today, the word 'newspeak' might well be on his lips. For, surely, what anchors our descriptions of things and events in the world is, precisely, the communal back and forth of stories about the world in which we strive to reach some form of working agreement. And isn't this why the conversations we have must be as wide, as well-informed, as inclusive, as multi-dimensional, as *democratic* as possible?

Many of us would want to say that the intellectual impetus which guides Tony Blair is, most clearly, a politically Liberal one; yet the commitment to civil society, as the site of an ongoing agonistic, which so characterises the philosophy of Liberalism, seems curiously absent. Intellectuals, who might be considered to have some contribution to make to such social conversations, are damned as having nothing interesting to say. In place of political commitments, and the on-going process of informed arguments which should be a part of democracy, we get polls and focus groups (without, apparently, much attention to the psycho-dynamics of such resources), and a sense that this government lacks the human richness which springs from healthy and diverse social and cultural engagements, exchanges and conversations. Thus the sense of ersatz politics, of politics without depth, of glittering surfaces, shows and words hanging unencumbered by any terrific relationship to anything beyond, beneath or behind them - of, as our theme names it, an impoverished one-dimensionality.

The essays here address various aspects of this one-dimensionality. Mike Rustin draws attention to the conflicts within contemporary ideas of modernisation - in the Conservative formulation of modernisation under Margaret Thatcher, there was a conflict between the radical, individualist free-marketeers and the moral conservatives; in Tony Blair's hands these conflicts were supposed to be overcome via the notion of the Third Way. But, argues Rustin, the Third Way is less an attempt to chart a course between market dogmatism and social democracy than it is an attempt to thwart conservatism from every quarter, left and right. We might see this as an attempt to reassert the liberal tradition of utilitarian radical social reform and sturdy individual independence which has developed since the late eighteenth century. In practice, at the beginning of the twenty-first century, what this entails is a wholehearted support for the market as economic and social system. But the earlier modernity, and its political manifestations of reform and change (and the eventual spread of democracy which they were inclined to foster), were supported by still entrenched religious and social values and networks, and recognition that democracy must be gradually accommodated; in contrast, contemporary neo-liberalism, as Rustin argues, exists in a very different context. Here, and lacking any truly *political* programme, the Third Way draws on other sources of value - most notably the market, the desires, means and ends of which then form an electoral programme. This, as I argue in my essay, is actually political choice masquerading as necessity. This realism, like all claims to privileged access to reality (which are inevitably tainted with the stale smell of authoritarianism), *must* contain errors - things which the future will judge as foolish. Arguing that it is the job of intellectuals to point to the possible fantasies of the present, by reference to developments in their various fields, I try to identify what are the follies of today, and find that they lie in the difference between the 'common sense realism' of New Labour TINA-ism and the rather different common sense demonstrated outside of the increasingly out-of-(democratic)-touch world of Westminster politics.

'Complexity', says David Byrne, 'seems to be an idea whose time has come'. Moreover it is an idea 'which not only allows for, but might be considered to require, political engagement'. Moving us beyond the politically paralysing value-crisis of postmodernism, complexity does allow us to know the world via the extent of our participation in it. Complexity implies that we know systems locally and by reference to context and history. We all know, for example, that, when a new person enters an institution, one of the commonest phrases they will hear as they encounter problems, obstacles or seeming mysteries is 'There's a history to this'. This is because we know, as actors in a complex system, that it is vital to understand contemporary pressures (contexts and resulting actions, etc) via their distinct, local and particular histories. Wide human communication is necessary because people in different positions within the system will have different 'takes' on these histories and experience various pressures in differently nuanced ways. What must be clear - and this continues the critique of modern managerialism and authoritarianism made elsewhere in this issue - is that human societies, and the micro-systems of which they are made up, can only function healthily with maximum creativity and adaptation when communication and participation in processes is maximised. Perhaps the contemporary mini-rash of TV programmes placing a group of individuals in (island) conditions in which they must survive on the strengths and communal vitality of the group evinces our growing interest in investigating the bones and musculature of healthy (or morbid) societies. Turning away from the story of 'downward determination' offered in conventional social science discussions of the global system, Byrne turns instead to the idea of 'nested systems'. Understood in this way the relationship between the local and the global is, more accurately, seen as running in both directions. Here, knowing how to change outcomes consists in knowing which parts (or groups of parts) of the whole system matter most in terms of the places where change is desired. For Byrne, the degree of inequality, and the differences which that makes right across a social system, is precisely such a 'control parameter', and it is directly linked to the concentration of economic power in the hands of capitalist elites.

Gavin Poynter's "'Thank you for Calling": the new ideology of work in the service economy' identifies some of the key constituents of the American model of service sector management theory and practice. The article argues that the rationalisation and routinisation of work typically associated with Taylorism and scientific management is being redefined and recast in the service sector context. Whilst Taylorism acknowledged the different (class) interests of management and worker, the new management approach to the rationalisation of work tends to blur the distinction. Management and workers, for example, are required to assume a common identity as 'service providers' and the recipients of services (patients, pupils, students) become customers. Whilst Taylorism concentrated upon the manual labour process, the new management approach focuses upon mental and 'emotional' labour, subjecting it to a process of routinisation through the use of such techniques as Business Process re-engineering (BPR) and Knowledge Management. Finally, whilst scientific management is often associated with the highly integrated 'fordist' factory, the new management approach attempts to flatten hierarchies and regulate relations between business units and work teams through a combination of internal markets and external audit. Poynter argues that while these new management techniques subscribe to the values of high performance and reward, in practice they achieve their opposite, not least - a point also made by Mike Rustin - because they encourage risk aversion and militate against original and spontaneous enterprise and innovation. Similarly, as 'managerial competencies' have displaced specialist knowledges as guiding principles in health or education, institutions have become driven by the requirements of a culture of audit, which displaces professional judgements of what is needful for the core tasks - whether of making populations healthier, or developing the intellectual capacities of whole individuals.

Barry Richards's 'The Real Meaning of Spin' sees a new late modern dimension in New Labour and other contemporary modes of rule, namely in the incorporation into them of specific techniques of emotional management.

He sees 'spin', and the personalisation of political leadership, as reflectors of a significant change in the social order, in particular the emergence of a therapeutic culture. Whilst some articles criticise New Labour for its one-dimensionality, it is important to see that several other contributors, like Barry Richards, are outlining new ways of looking at the political process – and exploring the complex emotional dynamics often brought into play. Some of the issues raised by Barry Richards link with an earlier *Soundings* issue whose theme was Emotional Labour, and we will be returning to them.

There is a high degree of agreement in many of the individual pieces appearing in 'One-dimensional politics' - and perhaps our readers will share much of the drift of the analyses offered here; they may also share our sense of moderated exasperation that anything so foolish as the system and beliefs currently prevailing in the Anglo-Saxon world of politics and big business could possibly have been wrought by human hands. Mario Petrucci conveys some of this frustration in his succinct fable. An obvious answer as to how this state of affairs has come about would involve taking note of the interests which are served by such systems and beliefs; a less obvious one might involve asking more troubling questions about the nature of the souls for whom material power is so satisfying that their connections to their less fortunate fellow human beings can be entirely disregarded and broken. But, in the end, perhaps the best answer to our collective amazement that things could ever have come to such a pass still lies with Alistair MacIntyre's analysis - now nearly twenty years old - in *After Virtue: A Study in Moral Theory*. MacIntyre argued that in the absence of a sense of lived, enworlded, virtue - of ethical commitments to what constitutes a good human life and good stewardship of the, always interconnected, social and natural worlds - we arrive at the goal of efficiency. When you can no longer state with any authority whether an outcome is good or bad, all you are left with is what MacIntyre describes as the managerialist goals of efficient performance - making the trains run on time: whether they are going to Eden or Auschwitz, and whether this is desirable or undesirable, just depends upon your point of view. In other words, the only counter to the ascendancy of the manager's values (or 'fictions' as MacIntyre describes them) is the concerted reassertion of human goods and bads. Managing *that* - which is to say talking about that, arguing about that, negotiating that - must be the central task we face in challenging a deadeningly one-dimensional future.

The New Labour ethic and the spirit of capitalism

Michael Rustin

Mike Rustin argues that the New Labour project, in its overwhelmingly pro-market stance, can be broadly interpreted as a variant (though a potentially more successful one) of Thatcherite modernisation.

Why did the new right's counter-revolution, against 'consensus politics', the welfare state, and collectivism, falter and break down in both Britain and America, just when it seemed to be carrying all before it? What relation does the emergence of the 'Third Way' bear to this foundering of what was in its own terms undoubtedly a politics of modernisation? Does it represent a radical break with it, or does it continue its essential project, in a different form? This is the issue to be explored in this article.

Different methods of modernisation

There was never any doubt that the Conservatives under Thatcher were committed to the triumph and modernisation of capitalism. Her fierce pursuit of the Cold War, her attacks on welfare and collectivist institutions within Britain and Europe, her fervent hatred of socialism, and her adherence to the economic theories of Hayek and Friedman made all this entirely plain. Much of the rolling Thatcherite agenda, for a time a state of permanent revolution indeed, was successfully accomplished. One can say much the same about the radical right under Reagan in the United States.

Yet, in both Britain and in the United States, this juggernaut lost its momentum during the 1990s. Conflicts within these New Right coalitions, notably between the radicals of individualism and the free market, and those with a conservative moral agenda, brought problems. Electorates which were responsive to programmes promising individual economic opportunities, chimerical or otherwise, were less interested in a new puritanism, seeking to regulate beliefs and personal lives. The conjunction of moralistic preaching by some, and the pursuit of a fast buck by others, within the same government or party (in the case of the Thatchers, even within the same family), brought the new right into disrepute in its later days. The resignation of Newt Gingrich, and the failure of the impeachment proceedings against Clinton, were as significant in this respect as the collapse of the Major government amidst accusations of sleaze and corruption. In the end the political style which had well served the purposes of smashing obstacles to the market, and to capital accumulation, was less well adapted to ensuring its positive preconditions. These included, for Britain, new forms of governance - in Scotland, Wales and Northern Ireland - and above all acceptance of the logic of European integration. So the Conservatives collapsed, and we started our journey down the Third Way.

The Third Way claims to chart a course for New Labour midway between dogmatic advocacy of the free market, and 'old' social democracy, with its allegiance to redistribution by elected government as its preferred means of reform. What is however becoming clear is that the Third Way is far from neutral between capitalism and its actual and imaginable antitheses. The essence of the New Labour programme is that it promotes capitalism, as an economic and social system. Thatcher's repeated proclamation that 'There is No Alternative' (that is, to the demands of the market economy) could as well be made by New Labour. New Labour differs from Thatcherism not in its commitment to capitalist modernisation, but in its different view of what this now entails. The objective of Thatcherism was to destroy the obstacles that had been set in the path of capitalism by decades of social democracy, welfarism and class resistance, This destructive work having been for the most part accomplished, New Labour has given the project of modernisation a more positive, constructive and socially-inclusive definition. [1]

'The enemies' of the capitalist ethic having been defeated (by the modernisation of the Labour Party as much as by the Conservatives' defeat of the trade unions and privatisation of much of the former public sector), it remains for New Labour to locate and incorporate new allies for this project, and ensure that it penetrates into every remaining corner of the national life. The necessity for this 'modernisation' is often rationalised in terms of the need to adapt, from the point of view of competitive survival, to the unstoppable processes of globalisation. This is largely a geographical term for the ever-more pervasive power of capital, operating through varieties of markets and technologies.

New Labour is unusual, among 'progressive' political formations, in having chosen to be the political and ideological representative not of the weak and the oppressed, those disadvantaged by the effects of market forces, but instead of the upwardly mobile and the successful. It is because New Labour has been so successful in convincing the upwardly mobile, in fact or hope, that it offers them many opportunities, and few risks, that it has reduced the Conservative Party to such disarray. With New Labour as the proclaimed friend of business, and with rates of return to capital far exceeding returns from wages and salaries, what need of a conservative opposition? What substantial interests are there left for it to represent? [2]

When Tony Blair excoriates 'conservative forces', and says he wishes to defeat them utterly, he has in mind conservatives of both right and left. The removal of power from the hereditary peers, the compromise forced on Ulster Unionism, and his commitment to the lasting defeat of the Conservative Party, demonstrate the former thrust. The continued attacks on the old left, and the resistance to the demands of public sector workers and trade unions, represent the latter. There are professional groups - the teachers, public servants - who fall into

---

1. The fact of seeing both Thatcherism and New Labour as being related to the modernisation of capitalism, and functional for it, does not of course imply that these regimes are morally equivalent, or that one is not far preferable to the other.
2. Harold Wilson in 1964 nearly brought off an earlier version of this coalition of the upwardly mobile, via his 'white-hot heat of the technological revolution'. However, his government was not able to give the same assurances to the powerful that their interests were in safe hands as New Labour is now able to do, and it foundered on these contradictions.

neither right nor left wing categories - but who are nevertheless attacked, in effect as conservatives of the centre. What all these negatively-defined groups have in common is that they feel threatened by 'modernisation', fear that they are in relative decline, and do not see much benefit to themselves or to their values coming from identification with the market.

The class divisions around which politics used to be organised were conceived as coalitions of the haves and have-nots, the better and worse off within the economic system. These were formerly conceived as structures of inequality, amenable to some degree to redistribution. Such material differences remain fundamental, but they have been recast in more dynamic terms, reframed as expectations of benefit or loss within a dynamic economy, not as how much or little anyone can be shown to have according to a particular statistical snapshot. Class coalitions are now being constructed in relation to expectations, not to mundane material facts.

Some have argued that this is a post-material society, producing and exchanging goods of less tangible and solid kinds than an earlier economy of material scarcity. This economy produces and exchanges not food, but cuisine; not cars, but particular designs of car carrying many symbolic messages to its owner and others; not houses for living in but as containers for lifestyles; not holidays from work, but temporary immersion in milieus which offer new identity props, repertoires, and adventures. These cultural concomitants of consumption were of course always present. What is different is that they have become a larger part of the point of consumption, and what feeds its continued growth.

Informational capitalism has its effects not only on the processes of production and consumption, but also on the political process. Politics formerly depended on experiences of deliberation and debate, on the articulation of collective solidarities and antagonisms. Representatives were appointed to further the interests, and represent the values, of those they represented. (Northern Ireland, for all its problems, still reflects such a political process based on well-defined social identities. Thatcherism, in its clarity about its friends and enemies, was also recognisably a political construction of this kind.) New Labour, learning lessons from the campaigns and governments of Reagan and Clinton in the United States, represents the triumph of a different concept of the political process.

Central to this concept is the question of marketing, hence the new centrality of public relations and 'spin' to government and party. [3] Politics ceases to be capable of generating and inspiring alternative values, or ends developed within its own sphere. Instead it packages and promotes values whose source lies in other locations of social power. The most powerful of these, within consumer capitalism, is of course the commercial market itself. Whatever has been constructed as desirable within the consumer market-place, as ends (relative wealth, pleasure, status) or as means to these (employability,

'class coalitions are now constructed in relation to expectations, not to mundane material facts'

qualifications, controlling the poor or deviants as threats or blemishes to the good life) is then promoted as an electoral programme. The vacuity of New Labour, and indeed the homogenisation of the political process under consumer capitalism generally, derives from the domination of 'economic growth' - that is of profit and consumption - as an end. [4] If the political process itself is attenuated, and if the main programmatic goal is to turn the public sphere into a more effective servant of the private and corporate, where is space left for political imagination and practice?

The answer, of course, lies outside the formal political process, in social movements, concerted protests like those at the 1999 WTO meeting in Seattle, in voluntary associations, in identity politics, and, as Laura Dubinsky describes early in this issue, in trade unions. A more pluralist constitution, with freedom of information, elected mayors, national and regional assemblies and the like, provides opportunities to articulate these autonomous areas of political action with the party process. New Labour however does not see them in this way at all, in a contradiction that bodes ill for its long-term consolidation as a force for enhanced democracy and dialogue.

British politics has been turned upside down, with left and right changing places in the constituencies they seek to mobilise. The Conservatives now most vehemently represent those threatened by modernising market forces, not their

---

3. The meanings of 'spin' are discussed in this issue of *Soundings* by Barry Richards.
4. It is this one-dimensionality of values that seems to have provided the principal imaginative problem for the Dome, and indeed for the Millennium celebrations generally.

beneficiaries. Those in their ranks closest to modern corporate enterprise, such as Clarke and Heseltine, have been pushed to the margin. The economic individualism and consumerism which its own programmes have made into dominant ideologies have eroded the structures of traditional authority and belief on which the Conservative Party used to depend. It is currently tormented by problems of how to adapt to a new libertarian culture which is the indirect product of its own economic philosophy. Not only was Michael Portillo defeated by a gay Labour candidate, but he then turns out to have had a gay past himself! Its best London Mayoral candidate chose to enjoy the affluent 1990s with not less than five mistresses! Shaun Woodward MP defects to Labour in part because of Clause 28 and the issue of equal ages of consent.

New Labour, meanwhile, itself functions like a modern corporation. [5] It is forcefully managed, well-disciplined, ruthless towards failure, and efficient in its use of the key modern corporate specialisms of public relations, advertising, and the management of its product-cycles. The products in question are policies, and the key to the political product cycle, which New Labour shows every sign of handling competently, is to make sure that the upswings and downswings of the economy, and the tax surpluses that this can generate, are in harmony with the electoral cycle. No-one seems to give the Tories much chance in two or three years time.

The capitalist ethic

Max Weber, in his matchless work *The Protestant Ethic and the Spirit of Capitalism* (1920-1, published in English 1930), identified for the first time the elective affinity between the self-discipline and rationality of Protestantism, and the qualities required to make capital accumulation possible. Capitalism depends on qualities of character, on norms and values, as well as on laws and markets. Weber perceived, through his understanding of Calvinism, the self-denial and

---

5. Anthony Barnett (*Prospect*, February 1999) has formulated this as 'corporate populism', which gives an apt new emphasis to the concept which Stuart Hall earlier devised in regard to Thatcherism, 'authoritarian populism'. In a valid contrast, Barnett juxtaposes the manipulative and authoritarian style of New Labour politics with the democratic pluralism he had hoped to see coming into being via a new constitutional settlement. What this argument neglects, however, is that corporate capitalism is the dominant driving force to which New Labour seeks to adapt British society, and that it offers it a model style of political leadership for this reason.

renunciation of material and sensory satisfactions that was necessary for saving and investment to take place, in capitalism's 'heroic' period. R. H. Tawney developed Weber's ideas, in *Religion and the Rise of Capitalism* (1926), describing the puritanical roots of the acquisitive and individualist ethics of capitalism.

The causal relations between ethics and economic systems are however complex and interactive. Christopher Hill's *Society and Puritanism in Pre-Revolutionary England* (1964) saw the disciplining and regulation of everyday life, and the attack on popular pleasures (the frequency of holidays and feast-days, dancing, the theatre and sensual enjoyment) as a means of inculcating the work ethic. Hill, writing from a Marxist perspective, saw this ethical development more as a consequence than a cause of the capitalist way of life. Edward Thompson's essay 'Time and Work: Discipline in Industrial Capitalism' (*Past and Present*, 38, 1967), and his discussion of Methodism in *The Making of the English Working Class* (1963), described a similar process of moral regulation in a later context. John and Jean Comaroff [6] have extended this argument to explain the social functions of Christian missions to the colonies, seeing them as all the more effective in transforming indigenous ways of life in rationalising and marketising directions because of their ethical intent.

There are thus many historical precedents relevant to the new moralities of modernisation. The figure of the Christian capitalist may be a more relevant model for understanding New Labour than the more-often discussed Christian socialist. These precedents also remind us that there have been other sources of resistance to capitalist conceptions than socialist traditions as such, and that these may need to be retrieved. A shopper in the Boxing Day sales was overheard saying that her mind was full of the previous night's film of *David Copperfield*, shown on television, and that it was making her wonder what she doing in this shopping mall. (She did however have in her arms a large collection of garments.)

From another twentieth century perspective, the writers of the Frankfurt School further extended and updated Weber's account of the 'ethic' of capitalist society. Drawing on Freud's critique of the repressive culture that Calvin had initiated, they saw that modern capitalism had need of a different ethic from that of abstinence and deferral. Marcuse in particular saw that

---

6. John and Jean Comaroff, *Of Revelation and Revolution* , Vol. 1 *Christianity, Colonialism, and Consciousness in South Africa (1991); Vol., 2 Christianity, Colonialism, and Consciousness in South Africa (1997).* University of Chicago Press.

consumer capitalism required the lifting of repression, and that mass consumption depended on the indulgence of desires of all kinds. In *Soviet Marxism* (1958) he brilliantly explained how and why the Soviet Union, in its phase of primitive accumulation, reproduced the puritanism and repressiveness of early capitalism. In *One Dimensional Man* (1964) he attacked the limits of a consumer capitalism, in which desires were unleashed, but nevertheless disconnected from deeper human capacities and needs.

Part of New Labour's originality lies in its return to this 'ethical' agenda. New Labour has recognised that a successful capitalist economy, in a global context, depends on the motivation of its people. Hence its commitment to remoralising the population, and in particular the poor, to inculcate in them habits of work, and a rational relationship between effort and reward. Its commitment to moral education as a key task of government is a major theme of Third Way theorists such as Geoff Mulgan, and explains Demos's interest in the communitarian ethical agendas of writers such as Etzioni.

Thatcherism in its earlier years embodied a straightforward ethos of ideological struggle against a perceived collectivist enemy, in which revenge for past indignities was a strong element. But once these battles were evidently won, the Tories under Major found it difficult to reorient themselves to their new position of dominance. The right, now ascendant, became destructively polarised between an amoral and cynical acquisitiveness on the one hand (represented by its various disgraced former ministers), and the fundamentalist, persecutory moralism of figures such as Widdecombe and Howard. (The tabloids effortlessly condense the two together, inciting indulgence only the better to condemn it.) New Labour's originality has been to see that the ethical agenda of competitive individualism relaunched by Thatcher, but clouded by her obsession with enemies within and without, was by no means exhausted, and needed to become the core of the next phase of political development in Britain. This is one of the senses in which one can say that New Labour is continuing the 'serious work' of Thatcherite modernisation, after the lull and diversion of the decadent Major years.

Thus, the essence of New Labour's concept of modernisation (like Thatcher's) is thinking in the long-term, planning, organising the future. (It is no accident that, like Thatcher, it had several terms of office in its sights from the start.) It is not (yet) a philosophy of 'get rich quick' - which was the pathological short-cut which many Thatcherites embraced - thinking of wealth as a spoil of successful class war, rather than as a reward for disciplined effort and foresight. Whilst New Labour positively embraces the accumulation of wealth as a worthy individual goal, it nevertheless recognises that wealth-creation depends on complex organisation, on interdependencies and linkages of many kinds. It knows that government is vitally necessary to this process, not merely as a battering ram, but as a constructive, enabling agency.

Whilst the main thrust of the Thatcherite state was destructive, aiming to dissolve obstacles to the power of the market wherever they were to be found, it also had its modernising, 'constructive' aspects, embodied for example in the reforms of the public services. Thatcher was able to live with forces more ideologically attached than she was to the providing state (Heseltine, Clarke) because of her inclusive and pragmatic sense of the needs of her whole project. The reforms of the public services initiated under this regime (regimes of constraint, competition, marketisation and regulation) have been softened under New Labour, but have not been reversed. It was only in the latter years of Conservative rule, as with the Republican right in the USA, that the contradictions between an ideological loathing of government per se, and its necessity in the era of global capitalism, became crippling. Major was chosen as leader for his incapacity to resolve these problems; Hague represents the choice of the reactionary pole.

W hat is striking about the New Labour project is how consistent and thoroughgoing it is in its conception, explicit and implicit, of how British society needs to be remade to be successful in the modern era. This sense that it is engaged in an epochal process of transformation, in many respects continuous with the changes previously set in train by its Conservative predecessors, is the source of its strength of purpose. The absence of debate about long-term goals, and any alternative options there might be between them, is striking. Figures previously identified with 'Old Labour', like Prescott, Blunkett and Dobson, have achieved no visible difference to any area of policy. John Prescott's deputy-leadership has a function for New Labour similar to Willie Whitelaw's for the Thatcherites, to protect its legitimacy with the faithful - traditionalists of the left in the one case, and of the right in the other. (The appeal of each lies (or lay) in their divergence; they came from opposite ends of the social spectrum from the middle-class modernisers of their parties - malapropism can be a political resource.) Mo Mowlam, at any rate a new and human voice, has been pushed to the margin, perhaps because she has the capacity to assert some different vision of politics. New Labour seems to be well ahead of Thatcher in the speed with which it is able to destroy and confuse internal dissidence. It is because of this pervasive uniformity of approach, and the silencing or disorientation of dissident voices, that the evoking of Weber's conception of a pervasive ethic (the ideological affinities and consistencies of modern capitalism as a system) does not seem misplaced in describing the Third Way.

What is New Labour's long-term project?

It is worth considering why New Labour has not so far explicitly disclosed its primary purpose as one of thoroughgoing commitment to capitalism and its necessary modernisation, proceeding rather by disavowals, negatives, hints, and arguments of practicality. The reason for this 'silence' is that New Labour has after all emerged within and from the Labour Party, which was set up to counterbalance, even supersede, the market economy. [7] Much of its support-base, both activist and electoral, still has leanings towards a different conception of what a social democratic party should be doing. The contradictions of this situation generate evasions and indirections, just as similar contradictions between old and new kinds of Tory did in the early days of Thatcherism.

Some argue that because the 'The Third Way' is so weakly articulated as a theoretical programme, there can therefore be no such programme. It is on this view merely a brand in search of a product. But an alternative explanation of this vagueness and indirection is to see it as a tactical measure, by analogy again with the development of Thatcherism. Crucial is the calculation of what it is politic to say, or even think, at a given time. 'Turning a blind eye' to certain realities can also have its purposes, in political as in psychic life, and exponents of the Third Way are adepts of the blind eye. [8] Thatcherism

---

7. To secure for the workers by hand and by brain the full fruits of their labour and the most equitable distribution thereof that may be possible upon the basis of the common ownership of the means of production distribution and exchange, and the best obtainable system of popular administration and control of each industry and service. (Labour Party Constitution, Clause IV (4) 1918 - 1995.)
8. 'Turning a blind eye' is discussed further in M. Rustin, 'The Future of Post Socialism', *Radical Philosophy* 74, Nov-Dec. 1995, pp17-27.

comparably evolved step by step, each advance disclosing the possibility of the next, in the last kind of permanent revolution that the left ever expected. Adversaries could never believe it was happening in so connected and total a way. But it was. Nick Davies recently established in an interview with Kenneth Baker about his reforms of the school system, which were intended to undermine the comprehensives (*The Guardian*, 16.9.99), how finely calculated at the time some of these steps were.

It may be thus with New Labour. We should ask where the architects of this project hope it will be in five or ten years time. (We should ask them to tell us.) What will British society look like? Will any major institutions live and breathe which are not either capitalist corporations, or quasi-public or quasi-voluntary organisations reconfigured to be as like capitalist corporations as it is possible for them to be? And if so, which will they be? What, for example, is New Labour's long-term vision for the BBC, and for the National Health Service (as Polly Toynbee, writing in *The Guardian*, has cogently asked)?

There seems no doubt about New Labour's preferences and prejudices. Whenever choices have emerged between the role of private corporations, and the public sector, however reconstructed, New Labour has leant towards total or partial privatisation. How else can one explain the intense resistance to the idea of keeping London Transport, or the air traffic control system, in public ownership? It must be that every such instance is seen as a local battle in a larger war. The London Underground has historically, after all, been one of the great successes of public enterprise. Most people acknowledge that the major cause of its recent difficulties is years of underfunding, a deliberate deprivation of resources introduced into the public sector by the Thatcherites in order to destroy public confidence in it. (The public sector can then be attacked, by both Conservative and New Labour governments, as if they have no responsibility for its failings.) The idea that part of London Underground should be handed over to Railtrack, of all corporations, is only intelligible on the basis that what was at stake was a major principle - 'private is better'. Something similar can be said about the semi-privatisation of Air Traffic Control. And why would New Labour keep Chris Woodhead, the witchfinder-general of the new managerial ethic, in his post as Chief Inspector of Schools, if not because it has decided it must defend every inch of an ideological frontier separating modernisers from the rest?

We have to ask also about the significance of the recent moves to introduce the private sector into areas of hitherto public provision or regulation such as schools and prisons. When a local authority, such as Islington, has its responsibility for the management of schools taken away from it, is this to be understood just as a one-off, an extreme remedy for an exceptional failure? Or, is it a first trial of the private sector in a new field, a testing-out or softening-up of resistance, to be later extended if the results justify it (although such evaluations are hardly innocent), or as and when this becomes politically possible? The Thatcherites have shown New Labour that it is possible to travel by incremental, partially-hidden steps. Since New Labour seems incapable or unwilling to make the case for public provision as having any distinctive advantages or virtues whatsoever, it seems prudent to contemplate the worst scenario in this respect.

The modernisation of the public sector

Then we have the pervasive transformations taking place within the public sector itself, under the rubric of the new managerialism, accountability, and audit. [9] What is involved here is the creation of regimes which mimic as far as possible the competition and discipline of markets. The problems that have to be solved to bring about this transformation are, firstly, to define management objectives which are as definite and measurable as the goals of turnover and profit which obtain in the private sector. Secondly, to establish contexts of competition which can incentivise relative success and failure, within the terms of these specified objectives. Thirdly, to enhance the power of managements over the workforces (of whatever salary grade), so that entire systems become responsive to the demands of these new regimes, and 'producer privileges' (e.g. protected and safeguarded conditions of employment) are reduced. (Gavin Poynter's article in this issue of *Soundings* explores these issues further.)

All these changes have been, or are being, successfully imposed throughout the public sector. Objectives and standards are everywhere made explicit - assessed measures of achievement by pupils in schools, quality of university teaching measured by inspection, 'best value' for local authority services, evidence-based outcomes of medical treatment. Some of these measures lead to a narrowing of, and sometimes diversion from, the primary

---

9. See Michael Power, *The Audit Explosion*, Demos

tasks; others (such as the outcomes of surgical treatment) are more beneficial. But a latent objective of achievement benchmarks in schools, or quality scores in university quality assessments, is to create measures or variables which can provide a basis for inter-institutional competition. Such competition has already been introduced for example for schools and universities. League tables of success and failure function like share listings for these mini-corporations, with the difference that it is the flows of their pupil clients, not buyers or sellers, which determine future values. These indices of performance, and the explicit competition that can be set up once they exist, are a powerful resource which managers can use to impose their power over employees, professional and other. The more insecure and vulnerable the organisation, the greater the scope for managers to enhance their power. The 'new universities' are for this reason much more heavily 'managed' than the old ones.

What is the benefit to capital in these changes to fields of activity in which it has previously taken little interest? The most obvious one is the continuous assault on the privileges, such as they are, of labour. Most of the gains of more 'efficient' management, whether in public or private sector, have come from downsizing and the more intensive use of labour-power. The size and compliance of the reserve army of labour, which contributes to low levels of inflation, is maintained by this continuing pressure on the public sector labour market. A second obvious benefit lies in New Labour's commitment to holding down tax levels, of which the constraints on and restructuring of the public sector are an outcome. The Conservative years saw a huge increase in the rewards to top earners, and in returns from the possession of capital vis-a-vis of labour power. The substantial empowering of the rich which was thus accomplished by Thatcherism will not be reversed by Labour's present tax regime.

There are two further factors. The first of these is that in an economy increasingly dominated by services, corporations need and wish to exploit the opportunities for accumulation in the service sector, as well as in the spheres of commodity production and finance. If these can be appropriately reconfigured, there must be large opportunities for profit making and capital accumulation in prisons, education and health. (We have already referred to the opportunities being given to private providers in these fields, the Private Finance Initiative being another example.) The ongoing issue of the role of the BBC reflects the same battles between public and private sectors in the spheres of media and information.

Unless there is a much more articulate opposition and resistance to them than has so far appeared, we must expect these trials to be enlarged and extended. They are the next frontier of the ongoing march of the corporate economy.

The final dimension of interest to capital in New Labour's approach to modernisation can be broadly termed ideological - something nearer to the 'ethic' which Weber saw, in its Protestant form, as essential to capitalism. The imposition of the disciplines of measurement, conformity, performance, reward and punishment on so many public sector activities hitherto somewhat remote from them, elaborates a regime, virtually a way of life, on spheres which used to define themselves as committed to values opposed in many way to those of the market. Blair's impatience with public sector conservatism is merely a less strident version of Thatcher's earlier visceral dislike of the public sector, which she saw as a hotbed of collectivism, dependency, and hostility to the profit-motive.

It is a paradox that the new forms of managerialist regulation being imposed on the public sector entrench further its inflexibility and one-dimensionality, relative to its private sector competitors. Interventions ostensibly intended to shift public provision into consumerist, responsive, mode, in actuality promote risk aversion, bureaucratic protectiveness, and slavish rule-following among public sector managers. Unfortunately, the models of corporate management selected for transplant to the public sector are often out of date before they even arrive at their destination. One effect of this imposition of quasi-market models is to increase the attractiveness, to those subjected to them, of the real as contrasted with surrogate market. If one is going to be managed, inspected, appraised, and resource-constrained to death, in a school or social services department, it might be preferable to be in the actual private sector itself. Difficulties of recruitment in public sector professions such as teaching, and the growth of private sector professions such as psychotherapy and alternative medicine, reflect these pressures.

'Thatcherism's substantial empowering of the rich will not be reversed by Labour's present tax regime'

When the 'soft economy' of human services is restructured in terms of measurable objectives and outcomes, what is at risk is the intrusion of the capitalist ethic into spheres hitherto insulated from it. Education ceases to be defined as the development of the potentialities of the individual, and becomes the achievement of measurable competences. Emotions, as we explored in our theme Issue 'Emotional Labour'(*Soundings* 11, become obligatory performances, required of cabin crew, shop-assistants, or counter-clerks, as a condition of continued employment. Since human nature cannot be remade to meet such requirements, divisions are imposed between public surface and inner reality. Employees are required to be friendly, but have never been more expendable. The depth of this crisis lies in the difficulty of imagining and sustaining alternative conceptions of a way of life.

What we are describing here is a reshaped capitalist ethic, a new 'dominant ideology' all the more powerful because it is being promoted by those who were formerly its opponents. Its 'puritanical' side lies in its insistence on obligation, the work-ethic, and the development of whatever capacities markets can find a use for. Its aspirant side lies in the seductions of consumption, and material success. The millionaire footballer or pop star, the lottery winner, the supermodel, are the icons of this society, no different under New Labour than under its predecessors. Its principal imagery is provided by advertising, harnessing every vital dimension of the human imagination to ends of selling, pervading almost every moment of existence. Its cathedrals, places of congregation, awe and adulation, are shopping malls. This is increasingly a society in which one system of values rules. This is the regime to which New Labour wants British society to adapt itself, for want of any alternative conception of life.

There are significant differences at least of emphasis between the accommodation to global capitalism advocated by New Labour in Britain, and the more critical stance towards it upheld by social democrats in other countries, such as France. Lionel Jospin, keeping his distance from 'the third way', recently argued for a strong regulatory role for government, as a necessary limit to market forces.

> We fully recognise globalisation. But we do not see its form as inevitable. We seek to create a regulatory system for the world capitalist economy. We believe that through common European action - in a Europe fired by social democratic ideals - we can succeed in the regulation of key areas, whether finance, trade or information … It is important that the features and

characteristics of our people, our history and our forms of organisation, are
not abandoned in this new world order ... This need to take control in
adapting to reality places a special responsibility on the state. The state is in a
position to provide the necessary direction, without taking the place of other
actors in society. [10]

What we should be expecting of social democratic parties is recognition that
capitalism does not have a monopoly on values, and that there are visions of
life and forms of power other than those determined by the goals of capital
accumulation for which parties and governments need to speak. Global
capitalism is latently totalitarian in its drive to control and define the entirety
of human life. The single-mindedness of New Labour, and its intolerance of all
voices other than its own, shows it to be in the grip of these invasive ways of
thinking, and currently incapable of contemplating alternatives to them.

---

10. Lionel Jospin, edited extract from *Modern Socialism* (Fabian Society), *Guardian*
16.11.99.

The intelligent process of living

Wendy Wheeler

*Wendy Wheeler argues that realism involves a
much more complex and sensitive view of the
world than is understood by the pragmatists of
New Labour.*

My title is taken from Christopher Bollas's *Cracking Up: The Work of Unconscious
Experience* - a book which describes the ways in which we know the world, and
especially other people in it, in intuitive ways which operate below the level of
conscious reasonings. [1] In this book, as in another work I will refer to - David
Abrams's *The Spell of the Sensuous* - an intelligent mind puts itself to the task of
describing a kind of intelligent common sense which, unless we are quite ill, we
have all actually experienced: a sense of an engagement with the human (and
also the non-human) world which is not amenable to accounting in any
instrumental or reductive way. In other words, Bollas (a psychoanalyst) and
Abrams (an ecologist and philosopher) join other contemporary theorists of
the human mind and its capacities (such as neuroscientists Gerald Edelman
and Antonio Damasio, biologist E.O. Wilson, and mathematician and Artificial
Intelligence researcher Keith Devlin) in arguing that 'common sense' is actually
rather more remarkable, subtle and significant than the 'realist' purveyors of
the idea - most notably politicians and businesspeople - like to think.

The problem I am trying to address here is this: the most direct 'doers' in
our world - the politicians and businesspeople who move money and policies
around, and affect our lives in very direct ways - seem also often to be the most

1. C. Bollas, *Cracking Up: The Work of Unconscious Experience*, Routledge 1995.

crass and unsubtle people, whose view of reality is of the grossest and most insensible kind. I do not wish to take the Platonic line of arguing that the ideal republic should be ruled by philosopher-kings; but I do think that things might be better than they are if the most material grubbers and fixers - the most *criminal* amongst us - were better informed about the 'common sense' of most human perceptions and relationships. Evidently, to be a grubber or a fixer means that you must desensitise yourself - via vast doses of statistics and utilitarian realism - to the way the world *really* is. The realism of the so-called pragmatists is, I will suggest, actually a foolish and limited *fantasy* of reality. Reality - to which genuine realists should most certainly apply themselves - is much more complex and subtle. Reality, and a true realism, await discovery. The reality of the Scholastics, and the Greeks before them, included the gods; the reality of Isaac Newton included alchemy; the reality of the Victorians included spiritualism. What unreality does the realism of today's pragmatists include? This essay, thus, takes the form of an extended question to Tony Blair - supposed idealist and Christian thinker, but actual pragmatic 'realist' whose conscience is hard to fathom - about the world, and its future, as he imagines it. For, actually, Mr T's political instantiation of the idea that There Is No Alternative is actually a fabulous fantasy; in the name of realism (modernise or perish! Reinvent yourself continually as saleable commodity! Play the global market-place!), the principled prime minister tells us that there are no principles capable of opposing, or even effectively managing, capitalism and all its manifold flaws.

I would like to put a question to Tony Blair. My question is: 'Do you think the world will be the same, a hundred years on, as it is now? And if the answer is, as it must be, "No", can you tell me how you think it will be?'. For it seems to me that in contemporary life, in the name of realism, there is a terrible absence of utopian vision, and of ideas and ideology in the best sense. The current 'realism' of TINA's 'modernise or fall by the wayside' has such a stench of either cynicism or economic partisanship that one wonders what kind of idiocy or tunnel-vision has got a hold of contemporary politicians. It is not that anyone sensible thinks that a utopia can ever actually be brought about. But a utopia is a guiding vision - never to be achieved, but always to be aimed at - of the good. When the word 'ideology' went out of fashion, or became risible, circa 1989, we lost a way of talking about ways in which one man's realism is another man's idea of hell. For fear of bigotry, supposedly progressive people have been happy to talk about the relativism of all values, but the unwillingness to name principled goods and bads has spawned a world in which goods and bads simply re-emerge with different names: realism is good; utopianism belongs to unworldly fantasists.

Are the political and business leaders of the Western world really so bold and vain as to assume that we have reached the peak of knowledge - that all history was leading just to us - or that the economic system which has grown to global dominance in the last decade of the twentieth century will, henceforth, exist throughout the rest of time? Is it assumed that, for example, all further scientific knowledge will be but an extension, in terms of methodology and the self-imposed limits of what counts as knowledge, of the kind of science that began with the seventeenth-century 'Scientific Revolution'? - and that the idea of what we call knowledge or science will not change? We laugh at the odd Victorian mishmash of earnest science which, one short century ago, could not tell the difference between phantoms and facts, and took seances seriously. Are we sure that, one hundred years hence, no-one will laugh at us? And if they do laugh, what is it about us that they will be laughing at?

The sleight of hand of our own times is to present economic fantasies - by which I mean the desires of the few - as the only reality. Political leaders of Western states argue that the current state of world trade organisation is the only economic reality for the foreseeable future, and that current policies must be formulated on this assumption; but this ignores the fact that change is, in part, brought about by a readiness to be convinced by alternative accounts of the future, or by political choices, and so on. To say 'this is how the future will be inasmuch as it is foreseeable' is to say 'This is how it WILL be'. This is political and ideological choice posing as 'realist' necessity.

The law of the world is Change. Things will not stay the same, and the proper role of politicians is not simply to manage economic necessity but also to facilitate change in the direction of the good. In doing this, governments might expect the intelligentsia to point to the limitations of current states of knowledge, and also to point to the areas where different and new accounts of 'how the world is' are emerging. A key task for contemporary intellectuals is to analyse the contemporary state of what Raymond Williams called 'the long revolution' - the changes which modernity brings about - and to point to the possibility that, eventually, what has been seen as modernity's 'dialectical undoing' (the ways in which real progress in some things turns out to increase man's bondage and alienation) might one day be changed. But intellectuals these days are largely undervalued, written-off as backward-looking luddites. They are not listened to - which is another way of saying that, damagingly, the political classes seem to be losing their ability to tolerate engaged criticism. As with managers everywhere, our contemporary political leaders (who are people who have lost the integrity of conviction which once went with the idea of political service) are unable to tolerate intelligent criticism. How proud, and how crass!

I would argue that the task of the contemporary intellectual is to identify the 'straws in the wind' of current scientific and cultural sensibilities, in which the 'mistakes' of the past are being recognised and rectified, so that intelligent political responses can be formulated.

Currently, change has three major aspects. Firstly there is the seeming shift, in terms of power, from nation states to multinational corporations, facilitated by the development of the e-wired global market-place; forms of global politics have emerged, as with NATO or the World Trade Organisation. (The latter, if reorganised along democratic lines, might conceivably return power to the constituent nations, and thus a different world agenda of greater far-sightedness and benevolence might be devised.) The second major change is the way in which the IT revolution opens up possibilities of political formations of local citizens reacting locally and globally against this currently undemocratic power. The third major shift is the final permeation of - and within - science itself by the spirit of human resistance to the 'mistakes' of modern science. I do not understand 'mistakes' as referring to the historic development of specific technologies; rather, the term refers to the conceptual context - the 'scientific world-view' - in which development takes place. In this new spirit of resistance (and also much aided by the power of modern computation), the mathematical, physics-driven, model of objective positivism is beginning to break down (as is the Cartesian separation of subject and object - the former capable of objective observation; the latter a 'given' capable of deterministic manipulation).

Straws in the wind

So what do these 'straws in the wind' tell us? What *is* it, in contemporary knowledge and science, which is manifestly incomplete? And where can we see this incompleteness being given cultural and political expression? Part of the answer lies in two strange words: enchantment and alienation. When enchantment is lost, alienation takes its place. It is sometimes forgotten that the father of modern science - Isaac Newton - was both an empirical scientist *and* an alchemist. The heritage of the scientist was to banish the heritage of the alchemist; but this did not mean that the concerns of the alchemist vanished. They merely re-emerged, in the form of a photographic negative, in the Marxian idea of alienation. When science - as a certain form of knowledge - banished religion and magic, and the intimate relationship between states of the body and states of the mind, the subsequent experience of being a human being became one that Marx would characterise as 'alienated': we no longer possessed ourselves, and the labour of our being in the world, in the ways which we had traditionally done; and, increasingly, the intimate relationship between our labouring bodies and our labouring souls was no longer given voice or symbolic embodiment in mythic forms.

This has, seemingly, brought us to the moment at which global capital claims its triumph; to the moment when we are told that There Is No Alternative to lives ever more 'managed' and ever less spiritually and economically secure, with the gap between the rich and the poor widening further. But at this very moment something is happening: voices and bodies are beginning to be raised against the unelected corporations, and the governments which are seen as not doing enough to tame them, and as acceding to special interests which are detrimental to most of the world's population. The spread of GM food is halted in its tracks by anarchists, greens and other concerned consumers; the WTO summit in Seattle brings numbers onto the streets not seen since the Vietnam anti-war demonstrations of thirty years ago; these people were there to object to the undemocratic nature of both the WTO itself and its outcomes in obliging countries to accept products (food with GM ingredients, for example) which their peoples do not want. For the three days of the talks, Seattle became a police state, and demonstrations in solidarity occurred around the world.

It is easy to see the themes in these movements: concern for democratic accountability; concern at greed-driven depredation of the environment and its creatures (including us); concern at political connivance in the protection of the rich and mighty at the expense of ordinary people. Through all this, more finely, runs an anxiety that the threads which are needful to bind a society - threads which must constantly tingle and vibrate with the million small and large signals through which a human culture remains in touch with itself - have snapped. These threads, when meaningful, bear the life of a culture's enchantments. For more than two hundred years, many many people in the industrialised and industrialising nations have felt the lines go silent, and become fewer and fewer - the sounds of alienation becoming the unheard scream which Munch painted. But with There Is No Alternative, we learn that the Big people have decided that the threads can be cut entirely. All sane people know instinctively that this cutting spells the end of society. They know there must be threads that bind, that the planet must be husbanded and that things which live and grow must not be peremptorily interfered with. Mary Shelley's *Frankenstein* had the immediate grip it did upon the modern psyche because it was recognised as one of the mythic figurings of modernity: of ambition and hubris so great that it could not recognise itself; of an aim at heaven whose end was hell. Shelley's monster did not read *Paradise Lost* for no reason.

One might say that the idea of holism, and the green movement itself, grew out of a general temper which recognised the threat that the threads might eventually snap; which understood that 'the web of life' (as Fritjof Capra has called it[2]) was under increasing strain - could be broken. This general temper has also manifested itself in other areas. The development of complexity theory in science (from flow mechanics and the mysteries of turbulence to evolutionary neurobiology to the human sciences and AI) marked a similar understanding - a sort of mathematically describable, computer-modellable, massive common sense. With these developments, linear determinism, the Cartesian distinction between mind and body, and the related distinction between rationality and the affections, began to be seen as false.

The funny thing is that the idea of reality which informs modern 'realism' is one which is almost entirely cut off from the kind of careful and very attentive realism which has allowed humanity successfully to survive for so long. This realism, as David Abrams argues, was one which obliged human beings to be extremely attentive to the sensuous living world of which they were a co-evolving part. Abrams describes the life of preliterate, oral and animistic cultures, and the ways in which the

---

2. F. Capra, *The Web of Life: A New Synthesis of Mind and Matter*, HarperCollins, 1996.

development of phonetic or 'alphabetic' culture made possible both a self-reflexive individualism and an idealisation of concepts which, with Socrates and Plato, began to uncouple ideas of truth, morality and justice from their basis in enworlded and local praxis ('the rest of life' or 'the life-world'); his argument is that we now need a curative return to the senses and their intuitions - a form of careful, enworlded and localised attentiveness. Following this line of argument, it seems reasonable to suggest, for example, that it is not the case that the experience of living in the modern world has killed our archaic dependence upon our sensuous intuitive life; rather, in suffering the sensuous battering of modern life,

'human beings have survived as long as they have because they have listened to their intuitions'

we have been obliged to numb ourselves (as Adorno intimated[3]). The search for informing sensation continues, but in ways made gross by the extent of the numbness to be overcome: 'Not least to blame for the withering of experience is the fact that things, under the law of pure functionality, assume a form that limits contact with them to mere operation, and tolerates no surplus either in freedom of conduct or in autonomy of things, which would survive as the core of experience, because it is not consumed by the moment of action'. In a recent essay in *New Formations*, Kate Soper fruitfully develops Adorno's theme in the contemporary context.[4] In the modern world, it is only in the attentiveness demanded by art, music and literature - in the face of which, and in order to be receptive, we must *slow ourselves down, be open and still* - that we rediscover non-alienated, sensuously responsive, being. Paradoxically, the aesthetic mode (which is also the mode of prayer) turns out to have most in common with the intense realism which, over most of human pre-history, has guaranteed our survival. As John Drury notes in a recent essay on Ruskin, 'He was quite clear - and surely quite right - in knowing that the basic reason for our enjoyment of art is that it gives us a piece of reality passed to us through the eye, mind and feeling of another human being with the technical skill and the courage to do it'; and, 'It seems to be an abiding human intuition, which he used abundantly, that penetration of the world at the point of one of its minute particulars will, if steadily and attentively made, reach into subterranean - perhaps even transcendant

---

3. See T. Adorno, 'Do Not Knock', in *Minima Moralia: Reflections from Damaged Life*, tr. E.F.N. Jephcott, Verso 1978, p40.
4. Kate Soper, 'Despairing of Happiness: The Redeeming Dialectic of Critical Theory', *New Formations*, 38, Summer 1999.

- universals. Any point in the web of experience, patiently scrutinised, leads beyond and away into the wealth of life. The self discovers other selves and the imagination at work cements society'.[5] Here is a programme still suggested by writers such as Abrams and Soper today.

Human beings have survived as long as they have, as the most highly adaptive species on the planet, because, over millennia, they have listened to their intuitions. Some of these have been problematic (the universal facts of racialised and sexualised inequality, for example - in which identity has depended upon a debasing of others on the basis of small differences - remains a problem to be tackled); but, unsurprisingly, many of our collective intuitions about the good are sound in relation to our understandings of what human communities need to survive.

When the BBC chose neuroscientist Susan Greenfield to give the last annual Richard Dimbleby Lecture of the twentieth century, it indicated an understanding of the great significance of developments in this field for the future. Here, it is science which is pointing to newly understood relationships between mind, brain and body in which mind is shown to be an emergent feature of a thoroughly embodied and enworlded brain, nervous system and body. With these developments, we come to understand that our affections - the inclinations and hunches which make up our intuitions - are integral to our reasoning. An ideology is - as Gramsci argued - a common sense (with the full bodily weight of everything which 'sense' implies) backed up by *power*. The sensuous life of the rich and powerful - which is to say their experience of being in the world - is gratified (or at least as gratified as an alienated sensuousness or *sensuality* can be) by the maintenance of things as they are; and these people, of course, have the power to argue that things should remain the way they are because There Is No Alternative. But this power derives from a wealth and influence which cuts its beneficiaries off from the truly *common sense*.

In Seattle in December 1999, as with the GM foods consumer protests earlier, it became possible to see another common sense and another intuition - that of the ordinary people of the world; theirs was a sense of increasing disenfranchisement, democratic deficit, and awareness that the 'common sense' of the world's elites was not their own. And, as a Gramscian might expect, this

---

5. J. Drury, 'The True Griffin's Eye - Ruskin's legacy: the virtues of imperfection, the refreshing violation and work as the spring of art and society', *TLS*, No 5049, 7 January 2000, pp11-12.

awareness, manifested in the peaceful protests of common sense intuition, was met with the force of the (unspoken) ideological state's protectors. The police response in Seattle was reminiscent of police responses to the miners strike in Britain in 1984; it graphically demonstrated the fearful response of the powerful minority to a public recognition of the extent of their undemocratic power and of the ways in which the world's political and economic elites *are* cut off from a general common sense of social goods. Just prior to the millennium celebrations in Britain, for example, I was struck by the news that the government - *our* government funded by *our* taxes - had put the police and army on standby in case of mass outbreaks of civil disorder. This is what our leaders think of us! And how misjudged! As might have been expected, and as noted by commentators in the event, the millennium celebrations were marked by extraordinary amounts of global and local goodwill between ordinary people.

At the beginning of this article, I posed a question about time, history and development to Tony Blair. This was a man who came to us in 1997 promising change. The whole country responded roundly: we wanted change! We did not want economic fantasists, we said; but we did not want TINA either. We wanted prudence and economic common sense, but we did not, necessarily, want an end to optimistic or utopian thought. And what is Tony Blair's vision for the future? Does it come with a little tinge of hopefulness, with regard for human intuitions and values attached? No. His vision is realism. The realist's package - complete with a craven attitude towards big business, and no economic policy other than that[6] - is sold as 'The Third Way'.

A change in the weather

So what is it that these out of touch political managers are unable to see and think? The straws in the wind - which herald a change in the weather - are much more substantial than the quasi-mystical 'third way'; and governments would do well to take account of them, to listen to the voices of the future, and to plot a good pilot's course accordingly. For this storm 'blowing out of paradise' is one in which the wreckage of modernity will be recomposed. For science, that bastion of realism, is on the point of overturning itself. In this

---

6. Charles Leadbeater, New Labour policy wonk, acknowledged this at the Number 10 Third Way seminar. See 'What the wonk told the PM', *Observer*, 10.5.98.

overturning, what counts as 'real' - positivist, objective, reducible to its constituent parts and manipulable - is changing. One might cite a social scientist, such as Zygmunt Bauman:

> Postmodernity ... brings 're-enchantment' of the world after the protracted and earnest ... modern struggle to disenchant it ... The mistrust of human spontaneity, of drives, impulses and inclinations resistant to prediction and rational justification, has been all but replaced by the mistrust of unemotional, calculating reason.[7]

But, now, one can also cite 'tougher' realists such as the neuroscientists and evolutionary biologists who present a very different view of human nature (and, hence, political proclivities) from that offered by either Benthamite utilitarianism or an earlier generation of biological determinists. Significantly, E.O. Wilson, whose nearly thirty years old *Sociobiology* suggested that genes are destiny, and that genetic manipulation might be put in the service of better societies, has shifted his view in favour of genetic conservatism and a 'holistic' and synthesising approach to understanding complex systems. His most recent book, *Consilience*, argues that it is incorrect to think of the arts and sciences as fundamentally opposed and that, via the rapid developments in neurobiology, it is increasingly the case that the old 'two cultures' will cease to be viewed as at odds with one another. Wilson reports a growing circle of artists and theorists of the arts who refer to their approach as 'biopetics or bioaesthetics', for example.[8] Christopher Bollas urges us to understand the very nuanced, not even conscious, communicative dance which characterises human relations (see footnote 1). Similarly, David Abrams alerts us to the subtle world of the senses which is drowned out in modern lives.[9]

The sound of the storm which will overturn the false realism which characterises the understanding of the world's current manipulators can be heard in the research mentioned above; but it is also found in the very many voices who question the wisdom of this limited materialism. Clinton and Blair may, as I have heard, be interested in the importance of creativity, and influenced by

---

7. Z. Bauman, *Postmodern Ethics*, Blackwell 1993, p33.
8. E. O. Wilson, *Consilience: The Unity of Knowledge*, Abacus 1999.
9. D. Abrams, *The Spell of the Sensuous: Perception and Language in a More-Than-Human World*, Vintage 1997.

the work of Mihalyi Csiksentmihalyi, but this is still seen - as in the 1999 Demos book *The Creative Age: knowledge and skills for the new economy* - as something to be put in the service of self-commodification for economic ends, rather than as something vital for our social survival and more profound ends.[10]

Various political economists, sociologists and historians - Will Hutton, Larry Elliott, Paul Ormerod, Richard Sennett and John Gray, for example - have challenged the economic short-termism of current arrangements within western, especially dominant Anglo-American, capitalism; but the charge should be extended to one of short-sightedness and inhuman insensitivity also. The rationalising virtues of Bentham unfortunately also included a distrust - noted by J.S. Mill in his largely sympathetic essay on Bentham - amounting to a rejection, of the intuitive goods of poetry. Yet, as Wilson argues in *Consilience*, the development of the arts, and of intuitive, subtle and interpretive 'aesthetic' (or 'sacred') understandings, have been as important to our survival as a species as any other branch of human endeavour.

For the time being, a one-dimensional view of reality - a limited, so-called pragmatic, instrumental realism - prevails. But, far from being 'realistic' in the sense of promoting human goods and survival, it is in fact hopelessly unrealistic. Millennia of successful human evolution have depended upon the maintenance of forms of knowledge (very often under the sign of the sacred, and of art in which a true realism is materialised) which are not reducible to instrumental forms of reason.

Modern forms of governance are supposedly influenced by utilitarian forms of research based upon statistics - and policy-informing research of this kind remains important. It might seem difficult to imagine hardened politicians and their advisers paying attention to intuitions; although, in fact, they probably engage in such things far more often than the 'hard realist' image portrayed allows. These intuitions - what someone recently called 'government by anecdote' - are problematic in that they may be ideological (in the bad sense) - apart from the fact that they are uninformed by properly informed democratic consensus and debate. The popular wisdom that the Tories remained in power for eighteen years because people are essentially greedy does not take sufficient account of either the degree of public ignorance maintained by British laws on the dissemination of information to the

---

10. M. Csiksentmihalyi, *Creativity: Flow and the psychology of discovery and invention*, HarperCollins 1996; K. Seltzer & T. Bentley, *The Creative Age: knowledge and skills for the new economy*, Demos 1999.

public, or of the widely-held intuition that the official Opposition was in too much of a mess to govern successfully. Government by focus group is no substitute for an informed public debate, and probably does not take sufficient account of the dynamics of small groups either. The current Labour government remains popular because of the perceived shambles of the Conservative Party, but many continue to worry about changes, in office, to Labour's pre-1997 democratic commitments (freedom of information; referendum on electoral reform, for example); yet it is precisely through enhanced and open information flows, and the presence of a wide range of voices and arguments, that a democracy may be able to find its own precious common sense.

We are currently in a period when large parts of the consciously calculable and reductive machine-logic of modernity remain alive, and when the arts and humanities (and even religion) face the attempt to reduce their values to skills and easily measurable 'outcomes' which can be 'managed'; but the future (provided we get there) will not be like this. Human beings are too imbued with the stuff of their evolution to allow this short, three-hundred year, phase in their cultural and social development to prevail for long. It is too destructive; and the insistence of the search for other values - whether via 'alternative' religions or therapies, or alternative political formations - indicates this.

The 'intelligent process of living' includes what E.O. Wilson calls 'the rest of life' and what Edmund Husserl and, following him, Jürgen Habermas have called the life-world. That is, the daily detail of life, which is excluded from significance in its own right and in its own terms (rather than those preferred and 'managed' by governments) by today's so-called realists. But 'the rest of life' *will* return because it is what human beings, through their evolutionary history, are made of. At the end of *Consilience*, Wilson says:

> I believe that in the process of locating new avenues of creative thought, we will also arrive at an existential conservatism. It is worth asking repeatedly: Where are our deepest roots? We are, it seems, Old World, catarrhine primates, brilliant emergent animals, defined genetically by our unique origins, blessed by our newfound biological genius, and secure in our homeland if we wish to make it so. What does it all mean? This is what it all means. To the extent that we depend on prosthetic devices to keep ourselves

and the biosphere alive, we will render everything fragile. To the extent that we banish the rest of life, we will impoverish our own species for all time. And if we should surrender our genetic nature to machine-aided ratiocination, and our ethics and art and our very meaning to a habit of careless discursion in the name of progress, imagining ourselves god-like and absolved from our ancient heritage, we will become nothing(*Consilience*, p333).

'Conservatism' here functions as a synonym for a certain kind of broadly socialist value - the value of conserving the human against the depredations of an inhuman modernisation. This is not a conservatism which resists progress in the manifestly good; it is a conservatism which understands that a progress which is not in tune with evolved human values is no progress at all. It is a socialist conservatism which recognises that 'progress' must be judged in human terms, and that the valorisation of the machine, and the inhuman, is a part of a fascistic socialism. The Nietzschean 'transvaluation of all values' requires a re-evaluation of old terms. This is the work we must do for the future. In the future, 'progressive' thought may be the thought which seeks to make a better future on the basis of a serious valuation of the goods of a long past. And through this dialectical contradiction, we may actually, really, move forward - in conformity with our ever-evolving human nature.

Conclusion

Finally, it must be clear that the terms in which we have couched our political understandings and affiliations in the past are no longer adequate to the new politics we need to make. To be radical, in the sense of 'tearing up by the roots', is only good when what is being torn up are the rank weeds which strangle healthy growth. To be conservative will be sensible when what is being conserved is healthy and time-proven. To be liberal is good or bad depending on who or what is, precisely, being granted greater freedom. To be progressive may be to pay more careful attention to the past. To modernise (itself a value-neutral term, neither necessarily good nor bad) may involve a regression and a diminution in the quality of life. To be a realist in today's terms may be to be a fantasist of the most deluded kind; and the sensuousness of art may provide a better model of knowledge, and a better guide to reality, than the gross sensuality of the politician or the profiteer.

Of course, from a philosophical point of view, observations such as these are not new: Feyerabend, Wittgenstein, and many of the philosophers associated with the Cambridge 'Apostles', have challenged the confidence of the hegemonic western scientific world-view. What is, perhaps, more recent though, is the extending and popularising spread of critiques of 'scientific reason' from within the scientific community itself. Today's political and commercial market rhetoric of 'reality' - of the triumph of global capital and the impossibility of alternative ways of economic and social organisation with different aims and values - has no greater claim to be counted as necessary and practical realism than had the pompous utilitarian self-congratulation satirised by Dickens a century and a half ago.

Things change. In January 2000, Jonathan Freedland wrote about the new spirit of collectivism being noticed by various observers.[11] Like all other commentators on contemporary cultural change, he noticed the importance of the web as a strikingly powerful medium of global communication, and the growth of consumer confidence. The massive resistance to Monsanto and GM foods and the demonstrations against the WTO in Seattle are recent manifestations of this new spirit. Given these developments, Blair's hectoring, top-down management style of government seems curiously misguided. Putting the Labour Party in government on 1 May 1997 was a collective act hugely collectively celebrated. People will not, I predict, be taking kindly to the Government's failure to recognise the power of the political consumers who put it where it is. Those who seek practical evidence of the truth of this claim need look no further than Ken Livingstone's massive lead in the polls for the London mayoralty. This isn't to do with policies; this is to do with punishing the hubris of the Thatcherite political mentality which led to the closing down of the GLC, and to the Poll Tax, which still lives on in Downing Street. How funny that the government and its unprecedented numbers of political advisers can't see what's right in front of them. The people, in general, are more empowered than they have ever been. A truly common sense, socially and politically articulated, has never been more possible than it is today, with the forces of history and the strength of a new technology leaning with it into the future. The power of the democratic customer on-line, in touch, joined up, will take on the mighty and bring them to account - and that means governments too.

---

11. J. Freedland, 'Us', *Guardian Weekend*, 8 January 2000, p8ff.

The politics of complexity

Acting locally matters

Dave Byrne

Dave Byrne argues that complexity theory enables us to think about more effective forms of radical politics.

'Complexity' seems to be an idea whose time has come. There are a range of books using the word as at least part of their title; and what amounts to a major new industry has grown up peddling 'complexity' as the latest trend in management guruism. Some of the scientists who have developed 'complexity' as a field make appearances at seminars which combine feeding the appetite of business for novelty with a genuine exposition of ideas and themes. I am going to argue here that complexity is more than the latest business fad, and even that it is more than a new project in science. Complexity matters because the central ideas which underpin the approach are the foundation on which we might take forward the left modernist programme of universal human progress. Complexity gets us past postmodernism as an intellectual project. It enables us to transcend the combination of destructive abstract intellectual rigour and plain political bone idleness which characterises the 'postmodern' academy, and to again recognise the possibility of meaningful collective action for social change. Moreover, and in Blair's Britain this matters a great deal, we can find in complexity a way of understanding the potential autonomy of local and particular action by people. We can recognise the mantra of global systemic determination as the ideological programme of disempowerment that it really is.

The best way to outline the essentials of complexity is by presenting a summary glossary of key terms. The first is 'non-linearity'. Complexity deals with systems in which change may be non-incremental and non-additive. The Newtonian programme of science is based on an understanding of causal effects in which the change in effect is proportionate to the change in the cause, and in which the effect of two separate causes is the sum of their individual effects. In complex systems, small causes may have big effects and there may be a failure of superposition. Causes may interact to produce outcomes which have no necessary relationship with their individual effects. The implications of these ideas were first discussed in general terms in Europe by the Nobel prize-winning chemical physicist Ilya Prigogine, working with a philosopher, Isabelle Stengers, in their book *Order out of Chaos*.[1] In the US a related but somewhat different programme has been conducted around the Santa Fe Institute, which is rather more scientistic in form and more closely related to the mathematics of chaos as such. It is a simplification, but not a gross one, to say that the approach of Prigogine and Stengers not only allows for, but might be considered to require, political engagement; whereas the US approaches suggest a technocratic and expert-led 'post-political' form of governance.

Complexity is about the behaviour of systems (a second key term). But this is not a question of the simple equilibric systems of classical physics, or that massively dominant programme in economics which derives from searches for Paretian equilibria; nor does it equate with the traditional focus of attention of cybernetics, the close to equilibric homeostatic systems in which negative feedback constrains radical change and system transformation. Complexity deals with far from equilibric evolutionary systems, in which the non-linearity and interaction mean that there is the potential for radical transformation of system form, with a range of potential outcomes - more than one but not infinite. Feedback is as likely to be positive as negative. Change can be qualitative as well as quantitative. Such change is evolutionary (key term three). Evolutionary change implies transformation through time in a uni-directional way. Complex systems have histories. It is important to

---

1.   I. Prigogine & I. Stengers, *Order Out of Chaos*, Bantam, New York, 1984.

note that such systems are complex and not complicated. Complicated systems can be described through a specification of the nature of their parts and of the inter-relationships among those discrete parts, and are vulnerable to any disruption of part or part-part relationship. Complex systems are much tougher. They can change in response to new conditions. They have the potential for adaptation to a new context. They are autopoietic (a fourth key term) - meaning they are self-organising. Moreover, in contrast with the closed systems described by classical physics or neo-classical economics, complex systems are open and real. They relate to an environment, and change in them may be in response to environmental change. It may also result from developments internal to the system. And it may result from the interaction of external environmental change with internal system disturbance.

The final key term is 'local'. Non-linearity and failure of superposition means that in a complex world we cannot have universal laws. We cannot establish descriptions of complex systems which hold always and everywhere. However, this is an ontological point, not an epistemological one. We cannot establish universal laws because in a complex world things change if context changes. This is essentially the same ontological position as that of critical realism, which sees the real as a domain of complex and contingent generative mechanisms. Indeed Michael Reed and David L. Harvey have persuasively argued that we should see Complexity as a scientific ontology which corresponds to realism as a philosophical ontology. [2] In a complex world we may very well know, but what we know is limited by context. We are not faced with the postmodernist epistemological dilemma of validating our knowledge claims. We instead have a real problem of identifying the necessarily local limits of those claims. [3] Nonetheless, we can know and, if we know, then we can act on the basis of that knowledge.

Human social systems are plainly complex - with that word carrying all the

---

2. M. Reed & D.L. Harvey, 'The new science and the old: complexity and realism in the social sciences', *Journal for the Theory of Social Behaviour*, 22, 1992, pp356-79.

3. In one of the clearest books on Complexity, Paul Cilliers (1998) argues that the identification of knowledge as local is compatible with a postmodernist account if the postmodernist account is understood as not absolutely relativist, but instead as validating only local claims. This is fine, although I think it would disturb many 'postmodernists' to have their story described in this way. P. Cilliers, *Complexity and Postmodernism: understanding complex systems*, Routledge, 1998.

burden of the account of complexity presented above. Actually, I think of the implications not so much as a burden as a potential. Complex systems can be changed, and changed by human action. One of the bases of such change can be knowledge of the systems themselves. Peter Allen notes of his proposals for modelling complexity that:

> It is somewhat disquieting to realise that the model we are going to build will contain the behaviour of actors, which will depend on the models available to them, which may include this one. That is why the aim of these models is not that of predicting the future. It is to help to understand the past and the present and the mechanisms which underlie them, and to explore possible futures so that they can be discussed and evaluated more clearly. The initial use of such models would be to help set the agendas for different actors: what would be a good or bad thing, and for whom. [4]

Michael Batty and Y. Xie put it like this :

> science is not simply about the study of actual phenomena but about potential or possible phenomena. This notion is central to design, but the prospect of a new science through computation which enables systematic and formal studies of 'possible worlds' has clear reference to the scientific understanding of human systems such as cities. [5]

We have to be careful here. Paul Cilliers contends that it is unethical to try to understand systems from outside - that we can never have enough external knowledge of a really complex system to produce a useful working model of it, however sophisticated our technology of representation, and that the kind of expert claims which 'planners' want to make on the basis of such knowledge can never

---

4. P. Allen, *Cities and Regions as Self-Organising Systems*, Gordon and Breach, Amsterdam, 1997, p178.
5. M. Batty & Y. Xie, 'Possible urban automata', *Planning and Design: Environment and Planning B*, 24 (2), 1997 pp159-64.
6. Cilliers, *Complexity and Postmodernism*. Actually Cilliers does say that systems can be modelled but he is uncomfortable with the notion that for really complex systems we can develop engineering style models, even if these models are understood not as universal scientific descriptions but instead as 'data compression'.

be justified on technical grounds alone. [6] This is an interesting argument and it suggests a different style of knowledge, of the need to know from inside, to know through participation in the world. I will suggest that Paolo Freire's arguments for dialogical knowledge, being founded on a programme of participatory action-research, offer us exactly such a way of knowing through being *and* doing. [7]

T here is one final idea from complexity which I think is important before we turn to a politics for the contemporary complex world. This is the idea of 'nested systems', which Reed and Harvey have taken from Prigogine and applied to the social world. I want to concentrate here on two socio-spatial levels - that of the global and the local, with the former understood in terms of Castells's globalised world system, and the latter understood as the range of local social action, organisation and culture in an urbanised world. It is very important to make the point that the idea of nested systems - which, in these terms, we can see as the global containing within it a multiplicity of localities, which in turn contain neighbourhoods, households, and individuals - is not a statement of hierarchy. In conventional discussions of the global system, as conducted in social science and as reproduced in politics, what we have is a story of downwards determination. The global sets the conditions for everything else. This is a story of global domination and local dependency. It is deeply disempowering because here the local can be as large as economico-political block (European Union) or nation state - the UK. Certainly no regional or urban level of governance and/or action in civil society has any autonomy in this framework.

This is not what the idea of nested systems implies. On the contrary, among nested complex systems, changes of causation and determination can run in both directions. Local actions can have global implications. That is a story of autonomy not of determination, at least in terms of potential.

Flexible but non-excluding - in your dreams but not in the world

New Labour has a clear enough political project. This is for the creation of flexible capitalism, in which innovation is not constrained by institutional forms, and in consequence of which we can experience continued economic growth;

---

7. P. Freire, *The Pedagogy of the Oppressed*, Penguin, Harmondsworth, 1982.

at the same time the population as a whole is both integrated into the new social system - a necessary condition for the maintenance of social order - and participates in the gains which derive from it. The potentially constraining institutional forms are those of organised labour in production, and corporatist (often catholic in origin) state welfare and employment mechanisms, including the traditional Keynsian tools of macro-economic demand management. What New Labour seems to want is laissez-faire and the combination laws, without pauperism. Of course we might, and indeed should, interpret 'Welfare to Work' as the analogue here of the New Poor Law. Blair and Brown seem to have pretty much the same belief system as early nineteenthth century utilitarians - let the system rip and it will all work out for the best.

I want to return here to the notion that, in transformations of the general form of complex systems - in their morphogenesis - we have more than one possible outcome, but that there is not a limitless range of outcomes. Some sorts of form are simply not available in the 'state space' within which systems can evolve. Although Cilliers has argued that we do not need to use the mathematics of chaos in understanding complexity, there are terms from chaos which remain useful to us. I am thinking here particularly of the idea of 'control parameter'. In a complex system, with all its complex and interactive local determinations – lots of things all going on together and all mattering – there may still be some things which matter more than others. And it may well be that what matters more is no single thing, but some combination of things which is nonetheless a much smaller set than that which describes all the characteristics of the system. If we want to change things we need to know what it is that matters in this way. By a rather crude analogy we might think of the control parameters as being like the knobs on a music centre, which we twiddle together to get the sound we want. We might be able to do more than fine tune here. We might be able to change things radically - put on another disc, turn to another station. This is a story of determination, but the word determination must not be understood in its usual sense in which it means exact specification of outcome. Instead we might think of determination, as Raymond Williams suggested, in terms of the setting of limits. That resonates very well with the general complexity account of human systems. The idea of control parameter(s) is a way of seeing what things matter most and therefore which things we might pick as the targets of social action. I will argue in a moment that the degree of inequality is exactly such a control parameter.

What I am going to propose is that flexibility requires both inequality and insecurity, and that no social system in which there is a high degree of these determinants, which of course interact, can at the same time be non-exclusionary. Sure, people may be ordered through insertion into work, but they will certainly be powerless, mere pawns on the board. Moreover, the cultural foundations of opposition, resistance, and transformation will be severely damaged in a social order founded on flexibility for capitalism and capitalists.

Exploratory scanning of the relationships among inequality, however defined, and the experienced character of the social order, suggests that inequality has a determinant force at all possible social levels. Richard Wilkinson's cross-national examination of the relationship between mortality levels and inequality indicates linkages at the literal level of individual life-chances. [8] Examinations of the changing socio-spatial forms of urban systems shows that basal resource inequality generates and sustains divided cities. Inequality seems to be intimately linked with the concentration of power in the hands of corporations and super-class elites in post-industrial capitalism. [9] Crucial to this inequality is the disempowering of organised labour through the recreation of domestic reserve armies of labour, and the liberation of capital on a global spatial scale, which is the foundation for the marshalling of latent reserve armies in new territories of exploitation. The insecurity which derives from the recreation of industrial reserves seems to be an essential attribute of highly flexible capitalism in all its forms.

Alongside massive exclusionary restructuring in the economic sphere, there is a simultaneous degradation of the traditionally effective mechanisms of democratic governance, especially at the level of local city regions. A central theme in Joel Nelson's description of post-industrial capitalism is that corporate power and the personally rich have acquired massively disproportionate influence over the operations of governance at all levels. [10] The consequence is governance by and for the rich. Indeed the dominant theoretical construct in contemporary examinations of urban governance is that of 'urban regime', which asserts that democratic processes

8.   R. Wilkinson, *Unhealthy Societies*, Routledge, 1996.
9.   J. Nelson, *Postindustrial Capitalism*, Sage, 1994.
10. Ibid.

are insignificant in comparison with the need for elected local governments to enter into 'partnerships' with corporations which control resources necessary for any policy innovation. There is a long history of this in land development, but the process is now spreading into service provision, especially in education and health.

Well, of course, we all know that under globalised capitalism TINA reigns supreme. There is no alternative. To which - from sound complex foundations - we might well rejoin as forcibly as we wish, and absolutely in the negative. The reality is that in the social world innovatory change at the local level can operate both autonomously (scarcely surprising when more than half of paid human labour - to say nothing of unpaid human labour - in any given place produces goods and above all services which are consumed in that place - *and* as the basis for change at the global level. Moreover, Freire's concepts of dialogical learning and participatory research provide us with an approach in which agency is embedded in the system being changed at both the local and global levels.

City regions are certainly complex systems, and tough old ones at that, but their contemporary form reflects the way in which local actors have subordinated themselves to the supposedly inevitable regulatory force of the financial flows of global capitalism. This is going to go a lot further than people thought if we don't watch out. David Price and his colleagues have shown how the application of World Trade Organisation rules to health care systems in which private capital has established any toehold whatsoever might open up the largest reservoirs of skilled and unionised human labour in the typical post-industrial city to transnational corporate control. [11] But there is no systemic inevitability about this - it is the result of actively passive political process. Politicians actively say that all we can do is be passive and accept these systemic inevitabilities.

Planners are turning to complexity as the basis of a set of technical procedures which might enable them to model and simulate cities as a technical exercise. One important incentive for this is that, in general, complexity-based approaches allow for inter-relationships between the natural and social worlds. In the context of cities, we have the possibility of linking ecological and social issues, particularly

---

11. D. Price, A. Pollock and J. Shaoul, 'How the World Trade Organization is shaping domestic policies in health care', *The Lancet* , 354, 9193, 1999, pp1889-92.

in relation to programmes of sustainability. The complex city can be directed towards both social and ecological sustainability.

There are real conceptual and ethical problems with this approach, but there is an alternative to the restoration of technocracy - with the technocrats in contemporary circumstances almost certainly acting as allies of the corporate sector. It is obvious that in cities today representative democratic forms are not working in either of the necessarily linked processes of coherent control over urban development or in the achievement of the popular objectives of urban people. It doesn't work for us and in most respects it doesn't work at all. The only thing that will work in a complex human system is the informed reflexive action of the people in the system themselves, including those with knowledge about the general form of such systems. Freire's conception of 'participatory research' is immediately relevant:

> Participatory research is an approach to social change - a process used by and for people who are exploited and oppressed. The approach challenges the way knowledge is produced with conventional social science methods and disseminated by dominant educational institutions. Through alternate methods, it puts the production of knowledge back into the hands of the people where it can infuse their struggles for social equality, and for the elimination of dependency and its symptoms: poverty, illiteracy, malnutrition etc. [12]

Here, experts can only be collegiate participants in empowerment: ' ... a consequence of liberatory learning. Power is not given, but created within the emerging praxis in which co-learners are engaged'. [13] The method must be dialogical: 'The dialogical approach to learning is characterised by co-operation and acceptance of interchangeability and mutuality in the roles of teacher and learner. In this method, all teach and all learn.'

Here we have a form for engagement with the real issues of our lives at the spatial scale - the local - where most people experience them. It may well be that the establishment of the office of 'elected mayor' for most UK 'cities' will

---

12. T. Heaney, http://nlu.nl.edu/ace/Resources/Documents FreireIssues.html# conscientization, p11.
13. Ibid., p10.

provide a platform for left/green coalitions to get 'Anti-Mayors' elected, people committed to the kind of collaborative and participatory programme of urban governance (and particularly of the establishment of strategic priorities) which a complexity account of politics suggests can be made to work. Indeed such forms must be made to work. Because nothing else will.

So to summarise:

◆ complexity provides us with the possibility of a systematic science for grasping the character of the world, but only if we understand that our understandings are necessarily local. Local, however, is both valid and useful.

◆ an examination of the character of contemporary capitalism from a complexity perspective demonstrates that a flexible unequal capitalism without social exclusion is not possible.

◆ planners are beginning to use complexity as a way of modelling the character of urban systems. However, the merely technocratic use of such approaches will be neither effective nor facilitate the restoration of democratic urban governance.

◆ A combination of the general perspectives of complexity with Freire's dialogical approach to social action offers the possibility of new forms of political engagement in the post-industrial world.

'Thank you for calling'

The new ideology of work in the service economy

Gavin Poynter

Gavin Poynter analyses the political and cultural implications of the managerialist restructuring of the service sector.

'Thank you for calling ... you are held in a queue at the moment ... press the star key to select the service you require...' The recorded message and the learned script of the call centre operator are repeated countless times a day in workplaces throughout Britain. The oral and digital routines of the telephonic interface shape the initial exchanges between buyers and sellers in many of the industries that constitute the contemporary marketplace. Call centres are the new front office or contact point for increasing numbers of customers in the service economy. The call centre labour process facilitates the twenty-four hour, seven-day week provision of transactions and advice. Britain has become the call centre capital of Europe with over 250,000 workers being employed, often on short shifts and flexible hours, in workplaces that share many of the characteristics of the controlled environment of the assembly line. A form of work organisation that was once the preserve of manual labour has rapidly diffused within industries that were previously associated with white collar workers and the exercise of 'mental' labour.

Call centres have provided a technical and organisational catalyst for the restructuring of many parts of the service sector. In those economies where the service sector has rapidly expanded alongside the relative decline of production industries, it has become increasingly necessary to ensure that productivity gains are secured to facilitate the maintenance of profitability and economic growth. Experimentation with new forms of enterprise and work organisation has enabled service industries to emulate labour processes that were once confined to the industrial sector. In the call centre, employees are subject to performance measurement and forms of work monitoring that obtain a level of management control and authority over the conduct of work that even Henry Ford would have envied. Indeed, close analysis of the interaction between the human/computer/customer interface typically reveals a level of manipulation of human relationships that places the exchanges, including the emotional signals, between worker and customer at the centre of the process of the creation of surplus value. Operators are trained, for example, in the verbal routines required to signal the end of a call. This is called 'effective signalling'. According to Aptus, a leading UK company that provides bespoke training packages for call centres, the adoption of this 'good' communication method saves seconds on each call and facilitates a significant improvement in productivity - reducing the length of each call by about sixteen per cent. [1]

The call centre is perhaps the contemporary form of work organisation that most exemplifies the development of 'effective procedures' to facilitate the manipulation of mental labour in ways that emulate the extensive routinisation of work that took place in many production industries in the first half of the twentieth century. The routinisation of service work is not, however, confined to those employed in call centres. Indeed, examination of developments across a number of service industries, public and private, reveals similar trends towards what might be called the routinisation of mental labour - or, as Kennedy has described it, the 'industrialisation of intelligence'. [2] The business imperatives that led to the adoption of assembly line working and other new forms of industrial organisation in the first half of the twentieth century have re-surfaced and been re-worked in the process of the restructuring of service industries towards the century's end.

1. J. Green, 'Save seconds: teach them how to say goodbye', *Call Centre Europe*, Issue 20, 1998.
2. N. Kennedy, *The Industrialisation of Intelligence*, Random House, New York 1991.

This article focuses primarily upon the management ideas and values which have underpinned the shift in focus of capitalist enterprises and institutions towards the demand for greater efficiency in the conduct of service work. The drive for greater efficiency has clearly discernible roots in the protracted process of industrial restructuring that has taken place within the industrial nations since the early 1970s. The productivity push has also, however, an ideological dimension, which has achieved a hegemony over hearts and minds - to the extent that its associated language and culture is not questioned or criticised either at work or within the wider society. This new form of managerialism provides the intellectual core of the modernisation project of New Labour; it pervades public and private sector services and enterprises and it articulates a set of values that are difficult on the surface to criticise. This article attempts to scratch beneath the surface. It explains the main features of the new managerialism and its origins in American management theories and practices. The article concludes with brief comments on the easy relationship between new managerialism and the values underpinning New Labour's third way.

Restructuring services - the emergence of managerialism

The American economy took the lead among the major industrial nations in developing an extensive service sector. The 1970s and 1980s were the decades in which a significant structural transition took place. Manufacturing employment stood still at around twenty million while employment in services grew at a prodigious rate. As the American economy faltered under the impact of increasing competitive pressures, particularly from Japan, the service economy came under closer scrutiny, with many academic and business writers arguing for extensive reform. Authors like Thurrow identified a number of reasons for the poor performance of the service sector.[3] First, in the 1980s falling real wage rates and low minimum wages relative to national average wage rates in many service industries provided a disincentive for management to use new technologies to displace labour. People were cheaper than machines but cheap labour also acted as a barrier to achieving greater efficiency through technological change.

3.   L. Thurrow, *Head to Head*, Brealey, London 1993.

Second, where technologies had been introduced they were associated with the expansion of management information systems and the growth of middle management layers rather than displacing them. Third, the growth of white collar bureaucracies had been encouraged by the development of hierarchical management structures in which individual managers received higher rewards if they were responsible for large numbers of staff. Middle management career prospects were, therefore, enhanced by a bloated bureaucracy. Finally, Thurrow argued that the growth of service industries like health arose primarily from the political failure of government to grasp the need to control health care costs. Thurrow's arguments were echoed by other business and academic writers, particularly in the lively in-house magazine of the American management elite, the *Harvard Business Review*.

While business writers made a strong case for extensive reform and restructuring of private and public services, economic instability and financial crises in the early and latter part of the 1980s made reform an imperative. The response amounted to a business revolution in US service industries, and gave rise to what Head has called a 'new ruthless economy'. [4] 'Delayering' reduced the number of tiers in the management hierarchy and 'downsizing' realised a reduction in staffing levels. Restructuring was designed to enable American capital to bring under control, arguably for the first time, those 'non-productive' areas of economic activity that were concerned with, for example, welfare provision, the circulation of capital and the activities associated with indirect labour and post-production work. The approach of American enterprises and institutions to restructuring involved five main elements: changes in management organisation and structure; the use of information technologies to reform work processes; extensive use of management consultants as 'external' catalysts of organisational change; the introduction of new approaches to employee relations; and the development of a work culture based on a pervasive 'customer orientation'. [5] A schematic representation of this model is provided in Table 1.

The US approach to service sector restructuring encouraged enterprises and institutions to shift toward organisational agility, reshape work processes and

---

4. S. Head, 'The New Ruthless Economy', *New York Review of Books*, 43, 4, 1996.
5. G. Poynter, *Restructuring in the Service Industries, Management reform of workplace relations in the UK service sector*, Cassell, London 2000.

Table 1: The American Model

Enterprise Structure	Work Organisation	The New Worker
Focus on core products/ services	Process not task-oriented	Performance measurement
Delayered/downsized	Software reshapes work processes	Performance linked to reward
Outsourcing support functions and discrete tasks associated with the service/ product supply chain	Polarisation between qualitative and quantitative categories of work	Individualisation of employment contract
	Competence displaces skill	Customer Orientation/ Internalisation of Management Values

adopt employee relations policies that encouraged the absorption or internalisation of 'customer-oriented' values.

The introduction of a raft of management philosophies and practices accompanied service sector reform in the USA. Organisational agility, obtained by breaking up previously integrated institutions into separate business units and budget centres, was referred to as establishing the agile or virtual enterprise.[6] The reform of work processes, using information technologies to redesign work, was codified into a set of practices that Hammer popularised as Business Process Re-engineering (BPR),[7] and Total Quality Management (TQM) practices were adapted from the manufacturing environment and applied extensively to a wide range of service work, particularly in the state sector.[8] The 'customer-supplier quality chain' became a central focus for the reform of public and welfare services. TQM, with its focus on the continuous process of improvement, refers only implicitly to productivity and efficiency within the institution or enterprise. Its primary purpose is the measurement and monitoring of the internal functioning of an institution and the establishment of criteria by which that institution may

---

6. J. Baker, 'Less lean but considerably more agile', *Financial Times* 10.5.96.
7. M. Hammer, 'Re-engineering work: don't automate obliterate', *Harvard Business Review*, July/August 1990.
8. I. Fitzgerald and J. Stirling, 'Quality in the Emergency Services: a preliminary discussion paper', Mimeo, University of Northumbria, 1995.

be compared to others within the same industry or sector.

These management approaches were accompanied in the early 1990s by the emergence of other ideas and values which sought to exploit more fully the potential of new information and communications technologies. Knowledge, according to the exponents of Knowledge Management, is information put to productive use within an organisation. Knowledge is explicitly stored in data bases and is also implicitly contained within the tacit knowledge of employees. It is sharing or externalising the latter that is a crucial element in enabling the emergence of a 'learning' institution that is capable of being competitive in the new information age. Knowledge management aspires to consciously exploit the hitherto 'hidden' depths of the individual in order to improve the market position of the enterprise. While call centre regimes seek to manipulate emotion for competitive advantage, Knowledge Management uses tailored software packages to capture the 'know-how' of the individual to achieve the same purpose.

The ideas and practices associated with the restructuring of the US service sector were rapidly seized upon across the Atlantic. Britain shared with the USA the experience of a rapid expansion of service industries and employment in the 1970s and 1980s. Equally, Britain also experienced the relative decline in manufacturing industry and employment, with the recession of the early 1980s dramatically accelerating this trend. On the political front, Thatcherism absorbed many of the underlying political values of Reaganism, and in the workplace management consultants became a useful conduit for the diffusion of the ideas and practices that had informed the restructuring of American service industries. In the National Health Service, for example, the ideas of Alain Enthoven, a Stanford University professor, made an influential contribution to the debate on reform. Enthoven was invited by Gordon McLaughlin, director of the Nuffield Provincial Hospitals trust, to spend one month in the UK studying the NHS. At the end of his stay, Enthoven provided the board of trustees with a report on the future direction that the NHS should take. Published in 1985, Enthoven's report argued for the development of an 'internal market' at the centre of which was the principle of the purchaser/provider split. His recommendations drew extensively upon US attempts to establish a more competitive, lower cost, system of health care provision through the introduction of health maintenance organisations (HMOs). As Day and

Klein commented, in their review of the reform of British health care, 'Enthoven's notion of the NHS internal market, to allow District Health Authorities (DHAs) to buy and sell services, looks remarkably like the solution adopted by the government four years later'.[9]

Emulation of the American model also took place in financial services. Indeed, it was financial services, the health service and government departments that made the most extensive use of consultancy services in the UK in the 1980s and 1990s. Major retail banking institutions adopted downsizing and delayering policies, along with programmes of branch closures and the consolidation of front office functions in regional data processing and customer service centres. These developments led Cressey and Scott to argue that the 'honeymoon' between management and workforce that had characterised management/employee relations in the retail banking industry in the post-1945 period was, by 1992, well and truly over.[10]

The subordination of service labour

White collar workers and the professions in the UK faced significant change in work organisation and industrial structure in the late 1980s and early 1990s . Mergers and acquisitions in financial services, and the inevitable process of rationalisation that followed, meant that all sections of the workforce were affected. Equally, in the NHS extensive reforms, including privatisation and contracting out, the introduction of Trusts and the reorganisation of the relationships between primary and secondary care, left few staff untouched. The extensive restructuring of service industries combined the de-centralisation and devolution of management responsibilities with the introduction of performance measures which evaluated the efficiency and productivity of business units and individuals.

Alongside these developments successive Conservative governments introduced a variety of semi-autonomous state agencies that were required to monitor performance at regular intervals in several key service sector industries, like health, education, financial services and central and local government. By

---

9. P. Day and R. Klein, 'Britain's health care experiment', *Health Affairs*, 10(3), 1991.

10. P. Cressey and P. Scott, 'Employment, technology and industrial relations in the UK clearing banks; is the honeymoon over?', *New Technology, Work and Employment*, 7(2) 1992.

the late 1980s and early 1990s the values of the 'audit society' were spreading fast, within a social framework in which a neo-liberal governmental philosophy rested uneasily with an authoritarianism that dealt forcefully with any forms of collective opposition from organisations like trade unions and professional bodies; the 'restrictive practices' of such organisations, according to government, presented a potential threat to the free operation of labour and product markets. The waning of trade union influence over workplace affairs, following the momentous defeats of the print workers and miners in the mid-1980s, with their implications for labour movement confidence as a whole, ensured that a new work culture could take root in service industries without incurring any significant countervailing collectivist pressure from trade unionism. By the end of the 1990s an instrumentalist and managerialist mode of thinking had achieved an unquestioned ascendancy in the service sector workplace. This ascendancy has several complex dimensions, of which three are outlined here.

First, employment contracts and the organisation of work have been reshaped around the central thematic of the 'customer-orientation'. The contractual relation between employer and employee has been overlaid by the marketised relationship between providers and purchasers of services, whether these relations are driven by competition between enterprises or arise from the demands of an artificially created internal market as in the NHS. For example, staff in service provision in local government, health and education feel anxious about the potential or actual threat of privatisation, contracting out, market testing and the necessity for efficiency savings; this then translates into pressures to contain costs and improve productivity, and encourages staff to collude with local management in attempts to 'prove' their efficiency - whether it be to external auditors, governmental agencies like the Higher Education Funding Council (HEFCE) or the local purchasing trust in the NHS.

Second, performance measurement has been introduced into these new market relations so that tangible and measurable outputs have tended to displace the less quantifiable and less tangible ones. This is particularly true of public services like health and education, where performance tables focus narrowly on criteria such as the measurement of patient throughput, the size of waiting lists, or the achievement of numeracy and literacy standards, to the exclusion of more qualitative evaluations - for example of a health service's ability to treat causes rather than symptoms, or an educational establishment's ability to develop the intellectual capacity of the whole individual.

Third, organisational reform has witnessed the introduction of leaner management structures, with new forms of management control being located closer to the work process. Managerial responsibility has shifted downwards, with local managers assuming greater responsibilities for budgets, personnel and marketing issues, while 'real' power over policy and strategy remains at the centre of the institution. Reform has blurred the distinction between the manager's role as a controller of the labour process and as a participant within it. In the health service, for example, qualified nurses increasingly combine clinical and managerial roles, while a growing proportion of nursing staff are employed on lower grades as nursing care assistants. Across service industries managers have been required to develop generic management skills and competencies, and their growing significance in the daily management of the work process has tended to displace or marginalise the position of professionals such as doctors or teachers. At the same time professional groups have become increasingly subject to the external scrutiny undertaken by 'quality' assessors. General practitioners are the most recent example of this trend, with government seizing upon the apparent failings of the few in order to introduce annual performance reviews.

The diminution of the professional's role in the work process within service industries has facilitated a trend toward the displacement of specialist knowledge by a range of managerial competencies. These are primarily concerned with the presentation and marketing of the product or service, rather than its qualitative contribution to the life or well-being of the recipient of the service. This de-skilling of professional work, and marginalisation of the influence of the specialist, has echoes of the expropriation of the skills of craft workers in late nineteenth and twentieth centuries.

Taylorism, managerialism and modernisation

The management ideologies that have informed the restructuring of service work in the late twentieth century have similarities to the scientific management theories of the early twentieth century. The appearance of the white collar assembly line, the marginalisation of the skilled professional and the subjection of service labour to quantitative measures of performance and efficiency all follow what might be called the classic scientific management model. There are, however, important variations from the classic prescriptions of Taylorism. Taylorism is associated with the separation of supervision and control from the actual conduct of work. But in contemporary service industries the trend is toward the devolution of management responsibilities to those who also do the work. Second, the growth of Taylorism coincided with emergence of the integrated, large scale enterprise (the fordist factory); whereas the routinisation of service work has been associated with the break-up of service sector institutions and enterprises into smaller business units and budget centres. Finally, and most significantly, Taylor and his followers recognised the distinct class interests and differences between managers and workers in the early twentieth century enterprise. But the key feature of contemporary management ideas and values is the displacement of the 'old' social distinctions at work – whether they are based on race, gender or class; they are now replaced by a 'new' set of social relations, based upon the superficial equalities of the marketplace, in which all participants become the buyers and sellers of services.

The old neo-classical world of buyers and sellers is now represented as a new world of providers and purchasers, with the state being primarily concerned with setting the rules and regulations for the effective conduct of market relations. The Blair project sits well with this narrowly defined, market-driven outlook. The role of government, for example, is to ensure that as many citizens as possible enter the labour market (the New Deal); and effective participation amounts to no more than the provision of educational opportunities to develop competencies that make the individual eligible for entry into the world of work (employability). The social agenda of the third way breathed new life into the market-oriented philosophy of Thatcherism. It at once absorbed its underlying values whilst at the same time representing the routinisation of service work and the marketisation of workplace relations as essential components of the policies designed to achieve the modernisation (or Americanisation) of Britain's service economy.

The real meaning of spin

Containment and compression in modern politics

Barry Richards

Contemporary spin politics involves specific techniques of emotional management, seeking to identify and contain popular anxieties, and involving the personalisation of political leadership.

Most people are now probably bored with 'spin'. Or rather, they are bored with stories about spin, with spin on spin as it might be called. The recent newsworthiness of the 'spin doctors' is fading. Some commentators may continue to find fascination in probing the skill base of this late modern profession, or in speculating on the scale of its influence. But for most of us the spin doctors and their works, while not going away, are settling into the background of political life, where we are told they prefer to stay, though they may occasionally be extruded again onto the front pages.

This is probably as it should be. It would be an unhealthy political culture in which the leading figures were primarily and constantly preoccupied with microanalysis of their impact upon the public. But it would be wrong to deduce that spin is no more than the narcissistic element in politics, regrettably inflated in this televisual age but really in the long run only a minor act on the grand stages of our public culture. Spin does indeed connect with the narcissistic tendencies which have a very long history in public life. But it also connects with particular modes of promotion and propaganda which have been most developed in the marketing and advertising industries in recent years; these have a shorter history but a much longer future, in both commerce and politics. Like other forms of marketing, spin is not a tasteless froth which can be skimmed off the 'real' thing. It is part of a change at the heart of contemporary politics, a change in the nature of authority.

To understand authority today we need to understand the idea of containment, an idea developed especially in post-Freudian psychoanalysis but finding application in a widening variety of contexts. It refers to the psychological importance of exchanges between people, or between people and social institutions, in which the anxieties of individuals are effectively managed. The process of containment requires firstly that the depth and nature of the anxiety is recognised and acknowledged by all parties in the transaction, and secondly that at least some of the people involved can confront and tolerate the anxiety. Their capacity to do so serves as a 'container' for the anxiety, and as a model for others. Anxieties that are recognised and tolerated are much less likely to distort judgement and to exert a negative influence on practical action in the world.

One feature of the present day is the increasing involvement of authorities of various kinds in the provision of containment. This therapeutic dimension to the exercise of authority has come about because we now inhabit a therapeutic culture, that is a culture characterised by a high level of concern with and investment in emotional management. To a considerable extent this is a work of *self*-management, since another feature of therapeutic culture is the fundamental importance attached to the self and its potential degree of autonomy. Nonetheless authorities are still needed, as sources of guidance and example for individuals in their tasks of self-management. Indeed, as these tasks are more fully engaged with, their scale and complexity is such that the need for authoritative help increases. The sources of it are often to be found in people and places we would not normally think of as being authorities in a more traditional sense of the word. For example, the work of containment by social institutions is now increasingly being carried by popular culture, especially by television drama, by the organisation of feeling around sport, and by popular music.

Positive and compelling images of authority are now of someone or something that can contain. Authority can be credible only if it has attuned itself to the anxieties of its subjects, if it is able to receive their anxious communications and to demonstrate how to live with their fears. Thatcher and Reagan were perhaps the last examples in the west of full-blown pre-therapeutic authority. In that passing mode, the tie of the subject to the leader was based not on containment but on its opposite: on the shared denial of anxiety and need, and on the projection of unacknowledged feelings into others who were then attacked for their weakness or their difference.

Certain issues can bring the process of containment - or the lack of it - into sharp focus. In what was probably his least well-judged statement since becoming Prime Minister, Tony Blair's insistence on one occasion in mid-February that genetically-modified foods were safe to eat, and that he was quite happy to eat them himself, completely failed to recognise the potential depth of public anxiety. Whatever health risks there may or may not be attached to GM foods, it has to be recognised that food can be a particularly sensitive topic in politics, as it can be in family life, because the infantile anxieties it can evoke will be very basic ones. A huge amount of trust is needed for the baby to feel that what it is being given to eat is good, and will not harm it, and when this trust falters, as it inevitably will at times, powerful fantasies of badness will be released. In its overall regulatory role in relation to agriculture and the food industry, the government perhaps comes closest to enacting the parental role in relation to the citizen-as-baby. Of course the National Health Service is also a prime site for the evocation of images of parental care, which is one reason why it has become such an iconic political issue.

Blair's comments on GM foods (like the Tory John Gummer's famous appearance with daughter and beefburger at the height of BSE anxiety) risked evoking fantasies of a crazed parent being prepared to sacrifice children to belief or self-interest, not images of a caring parent trying to understand and contain a child's anxieties however groundless in reality they may be.

Despite the Prime Minister's uncontaining contribution to the debate about GM foods, the present Labour government is more attuned than any other previous government to the new importance of containment and to therapeutic authority. Indeed this is what is new about 'New' Labour, aside from any arguable novelty in the substantive policies of the 'Third Way'. What is new is an understanding that political authority must henceforth seek to connect itself with the popular, in the sense of seeking to identify and contain popular anxieties. (One collateral strand in this was the much criticised 'Cool Britannia' strategy, if it was one, of linking with the containing institutions of popular culture.) In the late modern or therapeutic mode of emotional management, political authority must be popular, which is not to say that it will always stand in the position favoured by the majority, but that it is interwoven with popular culture and oriented to the recognition of popular fears and hopes.

This is the real meaning of 'spin'. Whatever the merits and demerits of the individuals best known for their practice of spin, the prominence of concerns with the 'message' is an indication of the importance now seen to reside in the management of the emotional dimensions of the political process. Like many other aspects of therapeutic culture, this prominence has been gathering since the 1950s, and - again like other therapeutic features - is (for obvious reasons) closely linked to the emergence of television. The moving images of wars, poverty and exclusion, and the fleshly presence of politicians in their inescapable personhood, which television brings to us all, have helped to bring the political process into visibly close entanglement with the emotional life of the individual citizen.

The much-scorned so-called 'focus group', that is the use of discussion groups of ordinary people to explore public attitudes, is in itself a neutral technique, but is potentially a means by which popular feeling and anxiety can be explored and identified, with the results of that inquiry being fed back into the intensified management of communications and therefore potentially to the work of containment.

The message of the 'spin doctors' - not the message they want people to stay on, but the underlying message contained by their activities as a whole - is that authority has changed. You can shoot these messengers if you don't like them, but their underlying message will arrive in other ways. Spin is the realisation that the exercise of political authority cannot proceed purely on the bases of rational argument about policy and the orderly contest of value systems. It is the realisation that political choices, like others, are now embedded in emotional narratives, and that these narratives are negotiable and subject to continual revision as they circulate in the public domain and move back and forth for each of us between the external world of newspapers, television, conversation and so on, and the internal world of anxiety, need and phantasy. Like other aspects of emotional life in a therapeutic world, they can be studied and - up to a point - managed. At the present time this function of political narrative management is located primarily in a poorly-regarded cadre of specialists within the political class. This, though, need not be its permanent location; it could become more integrated with other aspects of the political process, and no longer attract such specific and suspicious attention.

There is obviously another cultural trend operative here, alongside the therapeutic one. It is what the sociologist Andrew Wernick has called promotional culture, the increasing involvement of all social institutions in the promotional techniques of the marketplace. Spin is obviously about the promotional imperative when applied to politics, but the promotional imperative has to be understood in the context of therapeutic culture, because it is changes in culture 'outside' of the market place which determine what is valued in the market, and many social values are now heavily influenced by the therapeutic ethos.

In addition to the value of containment, a second key principle of therapeutic culture is compression. This refers to the way in which in late modern culture any specific social location can embody different psychic elements. One institution, or person, can represent to us, for example, both desire and restraint, pleasure and authority. This is a major difference from the compartmentalisation of psychic functions between different parts of the social body characteristic of the early modern period, when the carnivalesque of popular culture stood apart from the repressive institutions of church and state. There is now a compression of psychic functions at specific social locations: different, sometimes opposing, qualities are brought together rather than being segregated into different social spaces. To call this compression enables us to link it with the concept of time and space compression used in the sociology of postmodernity. In an influential description of postmodern society, David Harvey elaborated the concept of time and space compression. He argued that the development of modern transport and communication systems underpinned a radically altered experience of space and time, which lose their power to separate people and events and to maintain barriers and boundaries. In a similar way, and perhaps as a consequence of space-time compression, we can see a tendency for different psychic functions and agencies to be compressed and intermixed.

The outstanding example to date of this sort of compression is Princess Diana. No apology is due for prolonging the analysis of the Diana phenomenon - although some glib punditry and soothsaying may have poured forth in the wake of her death, the public reaction to it was one of the major mass-psychological phenomena of our time, and it may be some while before we can understand it adequately. In her persona were compressed an array of libidinal values - glamour, wealth, hedonism, anorexic neediness and so on - and a gathering of more superego-related ones such as compassion, world citizenship, and parental responsibility. This fusion of values distinguishes Diana from an earlier icon with whom she was compared. Marilyn Monroe's meaning for the public was rooted solely in the sexuality and emotional hunger which she embodied, without any countervailing values that might have endowed her with some elements of authority.

The compression exemplified by Diana is in the public image rather than in the inner life of the individuals concerned, though where the values combined are in extreme tension, as was the case with Diana, there may be considerable stress experienced by the individual concerned. As well as considering famous individuals, we can also look at trends in corporate imagery and institutional identity. Banks and building societies, once heavily clothed in images of prudent and restrictive authority, are now gaily bedecked with messages of pleasure and release, while also trying to retain some of the traditional functions of authority in the support and advice they proffer. In this as in many other examples, the compression can be seen to result from the increasing influence of consumer culture, drawing all sectors of life into its pleasure-oriented agendas; but it is important to note that the process is not one-directional. At the frontiers of consumer culture, in advertising, some recent innovations have seen moral and political agendas inserted explicitly into commercial messages, as for example in ads for film, biscuits, phones, and clothes. While one may be sceptical of the contribution of Benetton ads to the cultivation of global citizenship, the broad development of ethical consumerism is a substantial development which is having a major impact on marketing. It shows how consumerist hedonism is being tempered by its compression with moral discourse. In all these examples, from banks to Benetton, we see a compression of pleasure and responsibility, and a picture of how authority is being reconstituted in consumer culture.

There are other ways in which the domains of pleasure are being interwoven with elements of moral authority. Band Aid, for example, and the many similar ventures since, are a significant fusion of the libidinality of pop music with a rudimentary sense of global citizenship, of hedonism with a reparative wish. On many fronts, then, the sensual is becoming serious, and the serious is becoming sensual. Compression of other kinds of elements is transforming our society. Foremost amongst these would be the way in which, under the slogan of 'integration', many kinds of disorder and disability have been brought into everyday life, as with the attempt to include disturbed children or those with special needs in normal schools, and most controversially the strategy of returning the mentally ill to the 'community'. The idea of the 'community' as an inclusive, diverse and curative entity has put an agenda of compression at the centre of social policy.

Of course in the case of Diana and in other individual cases we could also note that there is a powerful narrative of *cure* at work, which is another feature of the therapeutic. These are people who are believed to have faced the demons inside themselves and overcome them. In the image of the damaged but recovered person there is both a central motif of therapeutic culture, and a key instance of compression. Images of vulnerability and resilience, and of pleasure and duty, are compressed into this kind of persona, which is becoming a prevalent type in present-day culture. While on the face of it we may seem in such cases to be dealing with purely charismatic qualities, and a revival of simple and dangerous charismatic authority, the compression of different psychic values into one persona means that in fact more composite and complex forms of authority are being developed.

L et us take these considerations and apply them to political authority. Ronald Reagan becoming President of the US could have been taken as confirmation of our most anxious predictions about the collapse of authority into its charismatic form: an actual star of the screen, whose only political talent seemed to be his ability to promote himself as likeable, was now the leader of the western world. But Reagan's sanitised image was too much artifice, and too simple. He marked the end of an era, not the arrival of one. Late modern spin is not about the preservation of an ideal artifice, but the management of complex emotional narratives. This is the difference between modern spin and more traditional manipulations of image, for which containment was irrelevant or antithetical, and compression a disaster.

How can we situate Clinton in this new cultural context? It has often been said in the last year or so that Clinton is a very 'compartmentalised' President and person; this refers to his ability to continue conducting the business of state in a focused way while often having to break off to attend to those aspects of his private life which have become public, not to mention attending to the consequences of all this within his family. However a more telling spatial metaphor would be that Clinton is a 'compressed' President, indeed is the world's first fully compressed national leader. His image has become an inseparable fusion of the political and the sensual; he is a politician still widely respected for his policies, especially domestic ones, and is also seen as a person of intense libidinal need. The libidinisation of the Presidency may have begun with Kennedy and his glamorous image, but in that time most of it was a secret. A great deal more sexual activity may have occurred in and around the White House then, but it was not in the public domain. In the compressed public culture of the millennial era, however, it is possible for the electorate to be as fully acquainted with the President's need for sexual intimacy as they are with his welfare policies, *and* for his authority to be undimmed by this.

'on many fronts the sensual is becoming serious and the serious is becoming sensual'

It may be argued that the electorate's continuing support for Clinton, and the consequent failure of the impeachment, expressed a popular decision that the private life of the individual is irrelevant to the discharge of public duties. Such a decision to bracket off the public from the private would not fit with the model of compression proposed here, because it would consign the personal sphere of sexuality back to the private domain, and demand that we cease to be interested in what our leaders get up to in private. This is not feasible; in this therapeutic age we are all too interested in what people feel and do in all areas of their lives. Rather, the continuing popular support for Clinton can be read as a forgiveness, an acceptance of the carnality of the President rather than an attempt to ignore it. It was a rejection of the prurience of the official inquiry into his misdemeanours. Sex is now forgiven; even using the office of state to secure indiscreet extramarital sex is forgiven. If there had been evidence that poor judgement in the conduct of extramarital affairs was linked to poor judgement in the conduct of affairs of state, the outcome might have been different. Some might want to argue that such a link must exist, but that argument appears to have been rejected by the majority. It has been determined that in the absence of such evidence, the President is allowed to continue as President, with a public image into which a profuse imagery of his disorderly carnal being has now been compressed.

To summarise, some predictions can be offered. I have been discussing two factors: the increasing importance of containment as a dimension of credible authority, and the increasing compression of public figures. These are distinct factors, but they are both part of the burgeoning of therapeutic culture, in which there is an increasingly explicit concern with the emotional self and its regulation, and in which a more diverse range of social institutions, including political leaders, have come to play a role in supporting emotional management. We can describe this in terms of a shift from a classical modern to a late modern mode of management.

In the political sphere, this shift means there will be more attention paid to the containing qualities of political communications, and that there will be more compression of public figures. The images, the public personae, of politicians will be infused with elements of the emotional and sensual being of the leaders as persons, and in the public domain a web of analysis, fantasy, judgement and speculation will surround these elements. Authority figures will be placed like everybody else in complex psychosocial narratives, in which strength and weakness, virtue and failing are closely and explicitly interwoven, and the everyday qualities of political discourse will come to reflect this. The same will be true of other aspects of the public domain; large commercial organisations, especially those involved in basic consumer provisioning such as retailing and financial services, will seek to acquire more compressed and containing corporate images, as consumer markets register more fully the changes in the nature of authority.

At the same time as public interest in the personal life of public figures increases, the threshold for demanding resignation over a range of issues concerning personal life will continue to rise. In a recent case when the disorderly carnality of a British government minister came to light, he was forced to resign.

Rightly or wrongly, the Prime Minister and his advisers judged that the individual concerned had lost authority, and might damage that of the whole government by staying in office. The loss of authority in this case though was possibly due to the security risk which was part of the story, not its libidinal nature, and we can expect that a compression of Clinton-esque proportions may soon occur in Britain.

Another phenomenon which this analysis would lead us to expect is the coming of a *damaged* leader, someone who as a person has been wounded and healed. Such leaders illustrate the principles of both compression and containment. People of this sort, in whom suffering is compressed with cure, can inspire a certain kind of confidence most powerfully. Their history of damage and repair can give hope that the leader can understand and contain the anxieties of others. The person who has been to the brink, or gone over the edge into illness or trauma and yet survived to lead a richer and wiser life, is potentially a model of resourcefulness and tenacity, and of how containing powers can develop.

The conventional fear that in the age of spin all politicians will be under increasing pressure to resemble a normative, antiseptic image of health and probity is therefore misplaced. Without underestimating the forces still around us pressing for the defensive construction of leaders as persons of pristine normativity, it is more likely that leaders of scarred identity and visibly flawed character will emerge, though crucially as persons they will be functioning as restored wholes.

Little Tony

Mario Petrucci

A new fable for new times…

Little Tony arose one morning on his little farm and realised he was lacking Community.

'I am so sad,' he said, tears welling up in his eyes. 'Everywhere here is so deserted. This must be a product of late capitalist neo-colonial de-ruralisation. I will go and seek a new Community among new friends.' And he walked towards the Big Smoke.

*****

On the outskirts of the Big Smoke he came to a great Crystal Palace built of glass and steel. Inside, Little Tony could see foods and delicacies of every imaginable variety, stacked as far and as high as the eye could see. Everything shone and glowed with health. 'Perhaps this is Community,' he said, and went inside.

There he saw a sacred plaque set in the wall and inscribed with holy letters. It took a long time for Little Tony to make out the words.

If you are in any way dissatisfied, the Manager will be pleased to see you.

Well, Little Tony certainly wasn't satisfied. After all, he lacked Community. So he plucked up courage and approached a young girl in uniform who sat painting her nails and occasionally ringing a bell. It must have been some peculiar religious ritual, because a very long queue of people stood watching her with a strange intensity.

'May I see Manager?' asked Little Tony brightly; and after about an hour, Manager appeared.

'Please, Manager. I hope you don't mind me asking, but is Community here?'

'Why, of course!' beamed Manager, and her hair was very tidy. 'This is the Global Community of Shoppers. Would you like to join us?' and she made a signal for Little Tony to be brought a bright new Trolley.

So, Little Tony Shopped. And Shopped. He Shopped all morning and he Shopped through lunch. He Shopped until it grew dark. At first, Shopping was fun. But then Little Tony began to notice that many of the foods came from places in the country where no-one lived any more, places that hadn't always been happy but at least had always been full of people. Not only that; although he passed many people who also had a sacred Trolley, no-one spoke to him.

'Hello,' he'd venture, brightly; but most of them averted their eyes, or said they would call for Manager. Little Tony wondered why they were so dissatisfied. Soon the Crystal Palace emptied, leaving Little Tony alone with Manager.

'Look here,' she said, eyeing Tony's mountainously filled Trolley and looking much less friendly than she had before, 'are you going to pay for all that?'

'What is 'Pay'?' asked Little Tony, whereupon two large men in uniform approached him and precipitated his rapid departure out of the Palace and into the night.

'It seems,' thought Tony, picking himself up off the tarmac, 'that you have to Pay an awful lot to be in this Global Community of Shoppers.' And he continued on his way.

******

It was nearly morning when Little Tony came to a magnificent glass building which seemed to disappear up into the clouds. It reminded him of the Crystal Palace but had more glass and looked as if it had been stood on its end. Little Tony was awe-struck. 'It's New, all so New!' he crooned. 'Perhaps *this* is Community.'

'Can I speak to Manager?' asked Tony when he was allowed inside. And after about six hours, Manager appeared. He was beautifully dressed.

'And what can I do for you, young sir?' grinned Manager through even, white teeth.

'Is this Community?' asked Tony.

'Why yes,' grinned Manager. 'This is *Corporate* Community.'

'I don't understand,' said Tony, which brought a sparkle to Manager's eye.

'Well,' he began, 'in our Corporate Vision for Society, everyone partakes of the Profits of the Company according to their pro-rata equivalent holding in Company Shares, with a negotiated percentile relief for overheads and advertising (in a highly competitive market) and tax deducted at source of course, and after gross deduction of my generous yet justified salary, naturally. How many Shares do you have?'

'None,' replied Tony, whereupon two large men in uniform approached him and threw him headlong out of the end-on Palace.

'It seems,' thought Tony, picking himself up again off the tarmac, 'that you need to have many Shares to be in Corporate Community.' And he walked on.

*****

By now Little Tony was cold and hungry, and not a little disheartened. It was just then that he came upon a vast Estate where strings of houses stretched away in every direction, tied together like daisy chains. In each house burned bright lamps, and families settled down to eat side by side on padded seats from which they watched a strange glowing box.

'Perhaps this, at last, is Community' sighed Little Tony, trudging through the gardens or pressing his nose to the window-glass.

The people inside grew indignant and shooed him away. 'We'll call the Law,' they growled after him. In desperation, he began to knock on the doors, one by one.

'I'm very hungry,' he said, close to tears.

A few people at least looked him in the eye, but they all either turned away or threatened to call the Law.

'This can't be Community,' sobbed Little Tony.

All at once, a white and blue chariot screeched to a halt mere inches from Tony's side. On top flashed an angry blue light. A woman and a large man, both in uniform, rushed out of the chariot saying: 'What do you think you're doing? We've had complaints about you.'

'Ah,' said Tony, 'you must be Law. I am very, very dissatisfied, which is why I suppose you are here. I am looking for Community. Can you help me find it?'

'We'll give *you* Community,' said the two in uniform, whereupon they shuffled him forcibly into the chariot and took him to a cold, dark place.

The Sacred and the Ethics of Living
Saturday 8 April 2000
10.00 - 4.30

We live in a society of secular individualism in which social solidarity has broken down - so how might we identify a new ethics of living? What might the relationships between individuals and society be? What is the relationship of these new ideas of community to the themes of class, identity, ethics, the politics of ecology, new technologies and popular culture? How might these relationships renew the collective impulse for economic justice, personal emancipation and democracy?

Speakers are: **Michel Maffesoli**, Professor of Sociology at the University of Paris, author *Ordinary Knowledge and The Sociology of Everyday Living*, **Giorgio Agamben**, Director of Philosophy Programme at the College Internationale de Philosophie, Paris and author *The Coming Community* and *Infancy and History: the Destruction of Experience* (tbc), **Professor Graham Ward**, Department of Religion and Theology at Manchester University, **Madeleine Bunting**, *Guardian* columnist, **Richard Holloway**, Bishop of Edinburgh, **George Shire**, Lecturer in Cultural Studies, Greenwich University, **Rachel Holmes**, commissioning editor at Amazon.com and **Wendy Wheeler**, author of *A New Modernity?*, and reader in English at University of North London.

Programmed in collaboration with Jonathan Rutherford and Anita Phillips

Tickets £16/£14 Concession £12 ICA Members.

For more information and tickets call ICA Box Office 0171 930 3647 With support from Middlesex University and Lawrence & Wishart.

Soundings

Described by the political theorist John Gray as a 'well written and welcome journal', Soundings is a unique venture that combines hard-edged political argument with a broad spectrum of cultural content. Recent highlights have included Stuart Hall, Jackie Kay, Gail Lewis, Mike Phillips and Lola Young on the significance of Windrush; Victoria Brittain and Basil Davidson on states of Africa; Chantal Mouffe on the third way; Angela McRobbie on the culture industries; and Bill Schwarz on the Tories; special themes have also included the European Left, Young Britain, Active Welfare and the Media.

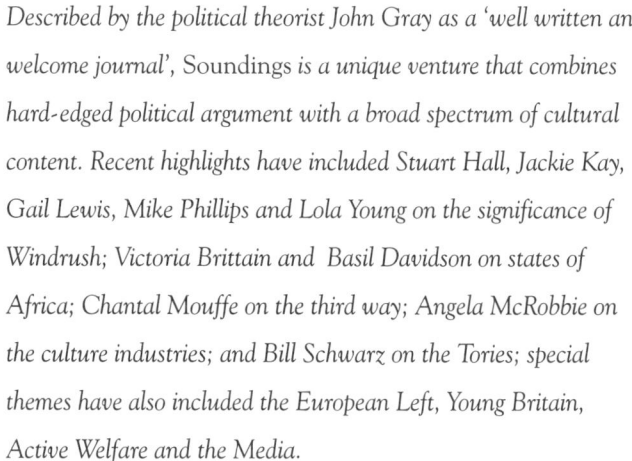

SPECIAL OFFER TO NEW SUBSCRIBERS

First time individual subscribers are entitled to a £25 subscription for the first year

Subscription rates 2000 (3 issues)

Individual subscriptions: UK £35.00 *Rest of the World* £45
Institutional subscriptions: UK £70.00 *Rest of the World* £80.00

To subscribe, send your name and address and payment (cheque or credit card), stating which issue you want the subscription to start with, to Soundings, Lawrence and Wishart, 99a Wallis Road, London E9 5LN.

OR you can e-mail us at subscriptions@l-w-bks.demon.co.uk